33 Minnesota Poets

33 Minnesota Poets

Edited by
Monica and Emilio DeGrazia

Nodin Press
Minneapolis, 2000

Copyright 2000 Nodin Press

All rights reserved. No part of this book may be reproduced in any form without the permission of Nodin Press except for review purposes.

ISBN 0-931714-88-5

First Edition

Library of Congress Number: 00-108260

NODIN PRESS
a division of Micawber's Inc.
525 North Third Street
Minneapolis, MN 55401

Printed by Printing Enterprises

Table of Contents

Melanie Richards
    When the Angels Discovered Grieving 15
    Maps of the Lost Kingdom 16–17
    Solace of an Evening Lit by Streetlights 17–18
    Dream of the Salamander 19
    White Tigers 20
    Nerval's Raven 21
    Dialectic of the Divided Self 22

Rob Hardy
    Girl's Night Out 25
    River Bend 26
    The Sacred Oaks 27
    Entomology (Will's Poem) 28
    You Were Never in the Army 29
    Morning 30
    Marjorie Rice 31
    Instructions for Silent Prayer 32

Peter Denzer
    I Live in a Crack in the Wall 35
    Tongues 36
    The Measure of My Life 37
    Coming Back from Le Havre—Spring, 1946 38
    No Metaphors 39
    A Light in the Night 40

Francine Sterle
    Still Life 43
    Second Sight 44–46
    Entering the Landscape 47–49
    Prayer 50

Eugene McCarthy
    The Public Man 53
    Three Bad Signs 54
    Grant Park, Chicago 55–56
    Place of Promise 57
    Kilroy 58
    Quiet Waters 58

Joan Wolf Prefontaine
- Earth Tones 61
- Raspberries 62
- Choreography 63
- Early Planting 64
- Tornado Salad 65
- Why I Pity the Woman Who Never Spills 66

James Togeas
- Austerity 69
- Scripts 69
- September Fog 70
- Angel of Belief 71
- Comet 71
- Empedocles 72

Linda Back McKay
- Ritual Branch 75
- Night Measures 76
- Indian Cemetery 77
- Dislocated Worker Project, Fairmont, Minnesota 78
- Responsibility 79
- The Barn Poem on Highway 19 80

Richard Broderick
- Equinox 83
- The Mountains of Florida 84
- Moonrise over Lake Michigan 85
- After Reading the Unabomber Manifesto 86
- On Moss 87
- Sundays Spent Working at Home 87
- Swimming Laps 88

Debra Barnes
- There's Talk 91
- The World Has Turned 91
- Out of Time 92
- Sonnet to Ravenna 93
- Marriage at 42 Below 94
- The Transcendence of Poetry 94

Michael Kincaid
- Northern Solstice 97
- Hymn to Otherness 97

    Lunar Function 98
    Orion's Promise 99
    Aeolian Oak 99
    Good Manners 100

Norita Dittberner-Jax
    Sauerkraut Supper 103
    Levitating toward Duluth 104
    Love Letters 105
    Classroom 106
    Senior English 107
    West Seventh Street 108

Jane Whitledge
    The Doll's Head 111
    Poet's Beginning 112
    Because My Father Worked Two Jobs 113
    Morel Mushrooms 114
    Summer of Flowers 115
    At the Wolf Kill 116

Steven Schild
    Beatitude: Cycle of Water 119
    Sandwiches after the Service 120
    Something for a Son 121
    The Bride 122
    Heirlooms 123
    At the Kitchen Table on the Anniversary of a Death 124

Kathleen Heideman
    A Field of Mudswallows 127
    Lost Gospel of Infancy 128
    Villanelle for a Negaunee Oracle 129
    How the Abandoned Lands Speak .130–131
    Come Sunday 131
    Signs and Signifiers 132

Michael Dennis Browne
    Hide and Go Seek 135–136
    Tree Care 137
    Evensong 138
    The Now, the Long Ago 139
    Mengele 140

Orval Lund
  Plowing 143
  For John, Who Did Not Choose Baseball 144
  Take Paradise 145
  Swede Decides to Quit Hunting 146
  Men in Winter 147–148

Bill Meissner
  First Ties: The Father in the Mirror .151
  The Father, Who Could Not Swim .152
  The Contortionist 153
  The Contortionist's Wife 154
  The Education of Martin Halsted 155
  The Secrets of America 156

Ethna McKiernan
  Homage to the Common 159
  The Other Woman 160
  Those We Carry with Us 161
  The Architecture of Flowers 162
  At This Moment 163
  In My Father's Voice 164

Robert Hedin
  Turning Fifty 167
  The Snow Country 167
  Waiting for Trains at Col d'Aubisque 168
  Bells 169
  Goddard Hot Springs 169
  The Old Liberators 170

Lucille Broderson
  White Milk at Daybreak 173
  Letter Never Sent 174
  Harvested Field 175
  This Is Your Old Age, Lucy 176
  At Seventy-Eight 177–178

Tracy Youngblom
  Release 181
  Sordid 182
  Joseph 183
  On Sunday Morning the All-Men Worship Team
    Takes the Stage 184

O Earthly Zion 185
Child's Drawing 186

Ken McCullough
Instructions (for Shivani Arjuna) 189
Visitation 190
Finishing Merrill Gilfillan's *Chokecherry Places*
    at the Cambodian Buddhist Temple, North Bronx 191
The Red and Black 192
Instructions (for Galway McCullough) 193
Run, Late November 194

Joyce Sutphen
Crossroads 197
From out the Cave 198
Launching into Space 199
Comforts of the Sun 200
My Father Comes to the City 201
Casino 202

Philip Dacey
She Writes Offering to Buy for Her Son,
    in Minnesota, an Electric Blanket 205
Badlands Love 205
Nomen, Numen 206
Counsel to the President 207–208
Walt Whitman's Answering Service 209–210

Mary Kay Rummel
Reading 213
Sonata 214
In the Night Kitchen 215
Burgundy Trillium 216
Medieval Herbal 217–218

Greg Hewett
Memorial Fountain 221
Turtle Music 222
The Distance to Birth 223
Hymn of 1978, the Last Word 224
Two Sons of the King of Delhi Hanged, 1857 225–226

Claire van Breemen Downes
Mulberry Creek 229

ix

Love Song at Evening 230
Postscipt to an Old Myth 230
Golden Time 231
A Double Sonnet in Honor of My
  Hundred-and-Twentieth Birthday 232

Margaret Hasse
Grave 235
Bean Fields 236
A Favorite Dessert, Lips 237
Lilacs in the Ditch 238
Marking Him 239–240

Anthony Swann
These Are My People 243
The Outpost 244
Beethoven Mad in the Streets 245
Wild Rice, Wild Roses 246
A Homeless Person Arranges His Belongings 247–248

Gary Holthaus
Brother 251–252
Blouse 253
What It Comes Down To 254
An Archeology of History 255
The Barn 256

CarolAnn Russell
Poets of the *Cimitero Acattolicco* 259–260
Hotel Excelsior 261
Last Judgment at Orvieto 262
Scala Del Bovolo 263
Incarnation 264

Scott King
At the Shore of Snowbank Lake 267
What It's Like 268
The Hill 268
Todos Santos 269
The Dark after Autumn 270
An Old Language 270

Preface

It may seem anomalous that along with a certain mastery of poetry the other criterion for inclusion in this anthology would have so much to do with the boundaries established when Minnesota became a state in 1858. Whether Minnesota-grown or transplanted, the thirty-three poets included here inhabit a *place* called Minnesota. This is different, of course, from saying that these poets share the same sense of place, or that they attribute any special importance to the settings where they live and write. Indeed these thirty-three live in locations so varied that the adjective "Minnesota" does weak service to the particularities of their work.

While Whitman's "leaves of grass" was an apt metaphor for his poetry, it is also a prophetic one for our own poetic culture. Most contemporary poetry is scattered about in the journals, chapbooks, and small press volumes which, taken as a whole, constitute a weighty grassroots presence. In the past three decades the growth of publishing and literary organizations and the proliferation of creative writing programs in our state have given credibility to poetry as a way of life. For good reasons Minnesotans take pride in the literary achievements of regional writers. Still, Minnesota poets are not household names, and the diffusion of their work to the margins of our cultural life in effect renders poetry and its makers apocryphal, or "hidden away." We are pleased to gather some of this poetry, along with unpublished work, and bring it to light in this anthology.

Of the thirty-three poets here who enjoy poetry as a way of life, some are well known in various literary circles, while others work without benefit of circle or conspicuous publication. The poets' brief statements about process and purpose provide interesting glimpses into their minds and hearts—glimpses that we trust will encourage readers and students to generate and sustain their own creative impulses.

Monica DeGrazia
Emilio DeGrazia

33 Minnesota Poets

(Photo by Mary Oberg)

Melanie Richards was born in a Salvation Army hospital near Milwaukee to a fourteen year-old unwed mother. Eventually she was adopted by her grandmother, recent widow of a painter and W.P.A. muralist whose painting of a sea monster offering a rose to an undersea woman was "my first brush with surrealism and the mysteries of the depths." After several educational adventures in Oregon and California she returned to a small farmhouse in Wisconsin, and from there moved on to the University of Minnesota. Her writing quickly flourished into publication, and she has won several awards for both her poetry and prose. As yet she has not published a book of poetry.

"My future," she says, "is unwritten."

When the Angels Discovered Grieving

"Human nature was originally one and we were a whole and desire and pursuit of the whole is what we call love."
—Plato

In the solarium of heaven
they wore robes of snow,
diaphanous, unlike our sixth grade
model kit of the visible man.

No blood coursed blue
through aorta and artery
into those still untroubled
hearts. No synapses fired

irreconcilable messages
from axons wired by longing
and insight and regret.
Their world a white affront

to the darkness without mercy,
without equivocation. The grey
did not yet matter, just the calm
of those pale androgynous limbs,

like marble shot with light.
No catch in the throat,
no blood run riot,
no lungs contracting

with the abrupt inhalation
that accompanies desire.
How could they know the price?
They were still whole and free

from longing, poised just before
that breathless fall from grace,
that hour when need and care
turn the untouched heart

Melanie Richards

human. Lost now, white feathers
blur in memory, the sense
of incompleteness
pushing them, arms outstretched

in that gesture of longing
that first came into being
when the angels discovered grieving
as they fell to earth.

Maps of the Lost Kingdom

She buys wild animals at auctions:
ocelots with pawprint fur,
miniature deer captured

in a Chinese rain forest,
a mated brace of ostriches
on a leash and, wrapped in moss,

the egg she cradles carefully,
smooth and cool and lonely
with the patience of the unborn.

In her dreams, Troy has fallen,
the last whaling ship sunk
at sea, the iron horse rolls

across Europe, flattening cities,
and in silence the animals rise.
Black oil drips in rivulets

from their wings, jeweled
collars clasp capes
of tanned human skin

inscribed with tattoos,
blue and familiar,
maps of the lost kingdom,

Melanie Richards

a land where the serpent spoke
and rent the air with ruin
and bathed the glistening

apple trees with regret.
She waits for the great city
to rise from the ocean floor,

temples inscribed with gilt
trim and carvings telling the story
of the end and the beginning

joined at last in each other's
arms, the man and woman
reaching tentatively toward each other

across the devastated orchard,
having lost the gift
of speaking to the animals.

Solace of an Evening Lit by Streetlights

Auguste Rodin / Camille Claudel

Because prayer was an expression of desire
and the world seemed at once impossible
yet just about to open to his touch,

he knelt amidst the wreckage of his days,
piles of dusty books half-read, every plate
unwashed, the cat's precise pawprints

across the papers on his desk. Open windows
invite the storm; curtains swell and billow,
the skirts of a waltzing, capricious ghost.

In the eaves, crickets dream, folding
small perfect violins under their wings,
bows glistening with beeswax. Their music

Melanie Richards

always a prelude, a celebration,
incantation of insects, a humming
transparency of wings. Orison of rain

against the rafters; purple horizon
like the dusky underside of plums, fragrance
of damask roses dying; the candle tallow

overflows. Green fire of absinthe. Thunder
and his pulse gone wild. Mastodons stirred
deep in tar pits as the primal mud

rose to silence Pompeii and patient
lava rolled like sorrow down the mountain.
What lasted was the woman's body

carved in marble, long hair pulled
to one side, white arms outstretched
in a gesture of longing or supplication.

With chisel and hammer, he captured
something luminous in her that held him;
held him though loss pinned his body

to the earth. Despite the weight of days,
at night he broke bread and said her name
as invocation of eternity, as invitation

to grief, as confession and as praise.

Melanie Richards

Dream of the Salamander

They have green tongues and are unforgiving,
molded on the seventh day of creation
out of afterthought and stardust
reflected in water, kneaded
by the rough hands of god,
and the salamander rises out of fire,
neither fish nor reptile, lost somewhere
before the categories came into being.

God must have looked up, tired,
and seen the sturdy bison
weighing down the endless prairie;
the giraffes adjusting their seven neck vertebrae
to the height of the African treetops;
flamingos poised tentatively on one leg,
flushed with color of tenderness.
He saw the zebras striped with ambivalence;
the gazelle grazing silently
in the luminous panels of sunlight,
and he dreamt of the salamander,
crawling up from his unconscious,
mud-wet, newt-like, a creature happiest
at the periphery because he could not choose.

To this day, I dream of the salamander,
red eyes unsettling my sleep. He comes at night
but not for love or any earthly reason,
sliding past the water weeds, webbed feet
making tracks like indecipherable hieroglyphics.
I see him now, poised in the final hour,
the sunset of the seventh day,
no single path clear in his heart.
Mud, sea, fire: his darkening firmament unfolding.

Melanie Richards

White Tigers

As though I could stop time,
I place in this box

a shell from that equatorial sea
where long-dead creatures

spiraled and dreamed,
a Chinese scarf the inexact

color of rain, and your letters
from Peru. You were solitary

and had just come down
from the mountain; I was nearly broken

by the life I'd left behind.
We were wary like white tigers

meeting in a clearing, each convinced
it is the last of its kind,

but that certainty dissolved
and was replaced by longing.

With dried orange rind,
fragrant sage, and a blue

branch of coral, I seal
this package full of artifacts

in case the wild horses
all vanish from the earth,

or the red throat of the hummingbird
lies to us about summer;

in case the manatees
blunder earthward and begin to walk.

Melanie Richards

Nerval's Raven

Through Paris streets, on a blue leash
he walked a lobster, tender
keeper of the secrets of the sea.

Women offered him the earth
splendid in its crown of peonies,
lupine, foxglove; offered him sleep

and the ancient dusky perfume
of the night, yet he refused
because of the ocean's salty

withholding music, because a woman's ghost
lifted pale arms to him from the mirror,
stepped away when he stepped away,

closed her eyes when he closed his.
With a single equation, he proved
the universe orderly, coherent;

the conception inspired, immaculate.
The night he died, rope tied
to a window grate, tongue swollen,

body limp, a raven flew in circles
over his head, repeating the only
words it knew: I thirst, I thirst.

Like the end of a contentment,
the newborn's first cry,
or the beginning of all desire.

Melanie Richards

Dialectic of the Divided Self

One was reaching out;
one running away.

One was backlit, burning, golden;
one black, dead black, alone.

One mended what was broken;
one was still busy breaking.

One was silky, tender, extending
needle, sheaf, shard or token;

one was bruised, dazed, frightened,
stubborn, mute and slow to ripen.

Melanie Richards

I recently discovered a new cheese at the St. Peter co-op, morbier, described as creamy, golden, the most sensual of cheeses. The label said the gray line in the center was a layer of ash. Like those painters who add a dash of the opposite to enhance the vibrant color they seek.

The complications of life, that inextricable braiding of grief and hope, inform the work of every artist. I think back to my younger self, so at home with a dreamy, visionary poetry. What's true is that the self evolves and the work along with it. Some times are fallow, others lavish.

Things to keep in mind: a Zen saying, "Great hope, great doubt, great effort." Sometimes one holds sway, sometimes another.

I do not trust intention; I'm wary of poetry without imagery and metaphor, music or mystery, uninformed by imagination. A poem is somehow irreducible, already in its purest state. The deeper poetic truth embodies the mysteries of our lives and mediates the visible and invisible worlds. Metaphor is how we make sense of our lives: some are given, some unearthed like precious ore.

A few of my favorite poets: Yeats for his continual ability to reinvent himself, Lorca the great magician of imagery, Neruda for his vast heart, Amichai at home in the sensual and spiritual realms.

So it's Amichai I'll end with: "I trust your voice/because it has lumps of hard pain in it/the way real honey/has lumps of wax from the honeycomb."

Lumps of pain. Lumps of wax. That hard-won, nearly imperceptible layer of ash.

(Photo by Heather Davenport)

Rob Hardy arrived in Minnesota in 1990 driving a rental truck loaded with the contents of a little graduate school apartment in Providence, Rhode Island. As his wife worked as a professor at Carleton College, Hardy became a substitute elementary school teacher and part-time classics instructor. But most of the time he stayed at home raising one, then two little boys, writing during their naps. In time his poems, essays and short stories began appearing in literary magazines. His most recent project was a new translation of Euripides' *Iphigeneia at Aulis*, which was performed by the Carleton Players in May, 2000.

Girl's Night Out

No matter how much I scrub or cook,
housework is never alchemy enough
to grant me temporary change of flesh—
I'm always the admirable chimera,
never resolving into my grosser parts,
or never escaping them. The facts are
the facts. Our flesh genders us
for different conversations and sex
becomes untranslatable, nuanced as it is
by the experience of our bodies.
A conversation about bodies themselves
can mean different things in and out
of the idiom of desire.
                        In short, I'm left alone
with the rhythm of the second hand
rubbing the clock toward midnight,
rounding to the nearest solitude,
nudging me closer and closer to myself.
Poor boy, with no story to tell of his first
period and likewise never knowing
with men how to begin a conversation
unless about a tool I need to borrow.
Could I get together with your husbands
and talk sensitively and with humor
about our first ejaculations?
It's not the same somehow, as if there were
poetry embodied in your moon rhythms
but not in the rough earthsongs we force
from ourselves.
                        Go sing yourselves back
into bodies and blood. I can only tune myself
to her body's hum, skirling out pleasure
like a round, becoming complete
with a voice sounding below and above.

Rob Hardy

River Bend

These places, like Old Testament miracles,
have ceased to exist, waiting for us
to recreate them. Like a prayer
the snow falls, my footsteps
scatter sparrows from the grass,
the ducks mumble over their pond. The prairie
cups itself to my ear, closes out the empty
stomach-rumble of the highway, and I hear
the grass voiced like an organ
with wind and birdsong, tongues of milkweed pod,
winter poised above me like a dark chord.

I come here with a heart in waiting
to learn the patience of seeds sleeping
winterlong above the frozen earth, the patience
of Sarai waiting to be renamed into flower.
This prairie is a covenant renewed
in the earth, a promise delivered
in the voice of fire, just as Moses heard
the voice of God in the wilderness. Here
I listen to the requiem of snow, the earth
awaiting the resurrection of its dead,
the whisper of wings making angels in the air.

The Sacred Oaks

The Dakota had no documents, no bones
or artifacts filed among the roots, no map
to enclose the trees within a numbered grid
of sacred ground. It was the same old story:

an oral tradition, stories told out like oak leaves
falling from disputed trees, becoming soil,
enriching nothing but this place on earth.

There was no telling the DOT that oaks
are sacred as lungs are sacred, their leaves
atoning in oxygen for the sin of highways,
or that their roots go back before treaties

into prairie earth, staking their own claim
against wind and fire, every ring around
the heartwood a notary's seal, a proof
of adaptation and survival. Now they are

gone, removed because they stood on a line
from A to B, the map's manifest destinations,
and in our haste to get there we could not
make a detour for the trees, or anything the earth

itself, without our human sanction, sanctifies.

Rob Hardy

Entomology (Will's Poem)

You came to a place where the woods, you said,
were pulsing with trees. Later, coming upon a pair
of grasshoppers immobilized in their stolid mating,

you told me that they were stacked like bunkbeds.
I sit for hours waiting on metaphor, like those
grasshoppers, paralyzed by the stubborn urge to create,

while you leap about in language, discovering
for the first time the pure ecstasy of words. This
is what I stopped to think. But you went to find a jar.

The grasshoppers looked so vulnerable, locked in their
secret knowledge, as if sex were an instinctual surrender
to death, but you thought only of the supreme pleasure

of bug-collecting, their pale-green bodies uncoupling
under glass. Like you, I often feel the urge to enclose
every natural act in some clear container, a poem,

something to remember by. You came of such an act,
such a longing to compose myself into something
separate and new, something I can no longer contain: You.

Rob Hardy

You Were Never in the Army

(To John Shaw)

When I won't eat the doubtful chicken delved
from the back of the up north refrigerator,
or the can of wintered-over beef soup, shelved
long past its expiration date, he says,
"You were never in the Army."

I don't reheat coffee the way he does,
in a small pan, as if helmet-brewed
over improvised fire, day-old, as it was,
or may have been, fifty-odd years ago
when he was in the Army.

I have never lain bloody in the cold Ardennes,
in the open sores of blasted snow,
nor have I stood at the old world's end
waiting to heal my wounds and build it new
after I was done with the Army.

I have no scars, and can never fall asleep
upright, as he can, as if I'd been marching
or waiting night-long in the anxious deep
of my foxhole—or merely at peace, having
nothing to do with the Army.

Rob Hardy

Morning

I'm not myself until I've had my coffee,
but the brown campesinos still complain
when I measure them into the coffee grinder.
It's too early for this.
For god's sake, I was kept awake
all night by the screams of the dark-
skinned woman in my closet who was peeling
strips of her own flesh to cobble into shoes.
All I want is peace in the morning—
not the pleading of ordinary things to consider
consequences, only the stillness
of the thing itself, the smooth earth-
and fleshtones of the coffee bean,
glabrous and infolded,
shedding a dicotyledonous shadow
in the light from the corner windows.
I could do without the clock
ticking off the children who died in my sleep,
the translucent whorl of fingerprints
stitched into the soles of my shoes.

Rob Hardy

Marjorie Rice

*A California homemaker who discovered
four previously unrecognized classes of
pentagons capable of tiling a plane.*

Her pentagons looked like houses
in the notation she devised—
a modest mathematical suburb
on California's tessellated coast.
In one house the stick figure of
a woman indicated the slide
and rotation of the angles,
as if she had inscribed herself
into her work, made herself
the symbol of a transformation:

because of the folding of sheets
and the setting of tables,
because of the daily reordering
of the same small pieces of her life,
because in dailiness she discovered
some idiomatic system of beauty,

her kitchen floor slowly puzzled itself
into a Moorish garden, as in Escher,
of hibiscus protracted into bloom.

Instructions for Silent Prayer

(To Heather Moody)

There is nothing more natural, the caterpillar
says, than to give birth to oneself—
to pull the chrysalis from your body's ragged sleeve,
folded in a glistening transparent stillness
while a deeper grace wings itself within.
It looks painful—skin split and contracting,
this straight-jacket escape, the body peeled away
to its volatile core. We never become less
physical by such decrements and involutions,
only more spiritual. What the body teaches us
to love becomes the spirit's cargo, wings
spread to gather up the body in benediction.

Most of my poetry arises from the same source as my perpetually lapsing Christianity, that is, from a sense of numinousness and from compelling unanswered questions. For me, prayer is an invitation to distractions, but poetry centers my mind on an experience, an object, an impulse which becomes more numinous in the concentrated effort to sustain and express that original impetus in words. I feel instant recognition when Maxine Kumin speaks of writing poetry as "an act of worship," as "a state of the soul," as "the scratching of a divine itch." Poetry is a compulsion, but is also a means of attaining at least a temporary state of grace, of working toward joy.

When I was diagnosed with mild depression, I realized that writing poetry was a kind of homeopathic self-medication. The impulse to write arose, I think, out of the same moody absorption, the same contemplative restlessness which, when unvoiced, expressed itself as depression. When I started taking an antidepressant, I found myself unable to write. I also found myself responding more enthusiastically to encouragement from friends to consider attending theological seminary. Interesting how my religion sought different expressions on and off antidepressants, the drug inducing a more conventional and unambiguous God.

Recently I've been going into my son's second grade class to work on poetry with the children. I once knelt down beside a little girl who told me she couldn't think of anything to write about. She was thin and frail, her skin like a candled egg. She had been in the hospital with a chronic illness, life-threatening, so debilitated that she was confined to a wheelchair. It made her tired to move her pencil across the page. Start with an experience or a feeling you've had, I said. I noticed the frightening scar on her neck from her recent surgery. Think about what makes you especially happy. Your mother, your grandparents, your cat. Write about that, your happiness.

She smiled and picked up her pen.

Rob Hardy

(Photo by Mary Denzer)

Peter Denzer currently spins his poetry while making pottery in rural Houston County, Minnesota. In his eighty year history he has worked as a cook, farmhand, private detective, bartender, and sculptor. His writing and broadcasting experience includes work for UPI, the Armed Forces Network, the BBC, and the American News Service. He has lived in Maine, New York, Detroit and Europe, including ten years in Florence, Italy that helped establish his "Renaissance Man" scope. During World War II he served as a political-intelligence expert and established the first independent newspaper in occupied Germany. On his return to the U.S. he published five novels.

He and his wife Mary operated a pottery shop in St. Paul before moving to rural Houston to continue their pottery work. There they grow much of their own food and cut wood to heat their home while being active participants in the community. Denzer has written hundreds of poems over the years, which he is gathering for a book to be published by Great River Review, Inc., in 2001.

I Live in a Crack in the Wall

In Naples a gecko on the wall is a portent of evil;
I don't know why.
There are also geckos in Hawaii
and spotted salamanders here in Minnesota
and in Maine.
Lovely green lizards darted in and out
of cracks in sun-warmed walls
around Medici villas
that looked down on Florence
where Medici no longer rule.

I am a lizard,
not green,
but white-haired and white-bearded,
living safe in a crack
waiting for the spring sun
to warm my blood
so that I can run about my metaphoric walls
and look down upon a metaphoric Florence
ruled by metaphoric Medici.

Peter Denzer

Tongues

All things speak to me
and I do not understand;
each stone or leaf
has its alien tongue.

Children hear voices,
some loud, some soft.
Deafened by cities,
insane thunder
of our wars,
they forget voices
heard when young.

I, too, forgot
and over years
learned the grammar
of daily ruckus.
Growing deaf to the racket
of our time,
I now hear voices
of leaves and stones and stars.

Peter Denzer

The Measure of My Life

Should I measure out my life by those occasions
when the indigo bunting sings its only song
and swings from a seed-filled stalk to feed,
or should I,
like all my mates,
count days and dollars?

I choose the bunting as it has chosen me,
coming into vision on days blessed by its fortune
and that blue confounding old memories of color.

Now all species are endangered
by my feckless fellow humans grubbing
in the flesh of mother's breast,
but no gold compares
to the bunting's sacred blue.

These creatures that paint the crystal air
of spring
with such holy hues
save the moments of our life and knit together
with airy arabesques
days past and days to come.

Prayers I say and praises sing
to these brief feathered fliers;
their time is mine and one more bunting means
one measure more of life for me.

Peter Denzer

Coming Back from Le Havre—Spring, 1946

Rats as big as my childhood's Cocker Spaniel,
and whores as ravenous as rats but not so well fed.
I was sick of Europe, Paris, City of Light,
and Gertrude Stein warning
"Beware the feather bed in Germany..."

She was right—war, conquest, defeat and sex—
all in the feather beds with lice, crabs, syph, the clap
and drunken confusion about who we were and why.
It was against the absurd rules of victory
to fraternize with the enemy;
Patton instructed his troops:
"Fuck 'em but don't talk to them."

In the brick tunnels of ancient French forts
overlooking a harbor littered by jagged remains
of sunken ships
a brisk trade in souvenirs:
Lugers, Nazi pennants, the buttons, badges, medals
Hitler's citizens could accumulate for services rendered
to the Third and eternal Reich.
A few more gruesome memorials, a dried ear
from among the effects of a concentration camp guard.
And more, until it was all unmentionable,
something bitterly evil sunk into fickle memory
and nightmares.

No cheering folks at the dock to greet us;
the heroes were all dead, stuck in VA hospitals,
in civvies looking for jobs or quonset huts
on college campuses swollen by GI bills.
New York City so clean, busy building;
"Business is America's business."

My mother shrieked when I came to her door;
she had never seen me in uniform
and none of my old clothes would fit.

No Metaphors

The lesion on my arm does not heal.
The medic soaks a cue tip in a cup of liquid nitrogen
and taps the lesion with the smoking cotton.
"If this doesn't work," he says,
"We'll do a punch biopsy."

I step from the clinic into brilliant warmth
for it is an exuberant May on the upper Mississippi.
The lesion, which may or may not be destroyed
by the deep freeze of liquid nitrogen,
is not a metaphor for the destruction of old cities.

My younger friend told me about his war.
My sister-in-law told me about her war
and captivity in one of Hitler's death camps.
I told my wife about my war.

Once, during a tornado, we cowered in a basement.
But a tornado is not a metaphor for war.
In this part of the world
We have tornadoes every summer.

There is no metaphor for war.

Peter Denzer

A Light in the Night

I got up to pee and felt my way through the dark
to the bathroom, noting on the way that there seemed
to be a soft glow in the room so that I could see
the empty place in the gloom where the door was.
When I got to the bathroom and turned toward the bowl
I saw a light in the mirror.
It came from my belly, just a bit above
and to the right of my belly button.

A glowing spot about the size of a quarter.

I probed the glow with my finger and felt nothing.
I rubbed the spot and thought
perhaps it glowed a bit more brightly.
I sniffed my finger and it smelled a bit like soap,
perhaps because I had bathed before going to bed.

I thought at first I was beginning to putrefy.

When I returned to bed, my bladder relieved,
I peeked under the sheet and the cotton cavern
was brightly illuminated by the spot on my belly.

I've said nothing about it to my wife, grateful
that in daylight I do not glow.

Peter Denzer

A poem is a statement clothed *in any one of the song and dance lines the poet learns, especially during childhood. The poet should take citizenship seriously and be able to address political, social, party and non-party issues. Who can better call for revolution, and who is better equipped to sense popular anger, fears and dreams? Who can better maintain sanity in the madness of chaos induced by despair, hunger and violence? Who can better say what we are for and why we live?*

Poets are free to use words that call up all elements of community, of life, of history, of politics, science, religion. There are criteria that must be met. A poem must be music, dance and drama; it must stir response in all the deepest levels of the flesh.

And finally the poet's cry is for the species' need for beauty; a poem should cry out against ugliness imposed on the planet's fragile life system by war, greed, and ego unhinged by fear and the mystery of beginnings and endings.

Okay boss?

Francine Sterle loves to travel, but her writing life is most intimately connected to her home ground in northeastern Minnesota. The author of *The White Bridge* (Poetry Harbor, 1999) and *Every Bird is One Bird* (Tupelo Press, 2001), she has won many fellowships and grants, and her poems have appeared in many literary journals. When she is not writing, reading or teaching poetry, she and her husband, a psychologist, facilitate workshops in the energy psychotherapies. She also cares for two geriatric cats and a two year-old Rhodesian Ridgeback.

Still Life

On the immaculate cloth, an arrangement:
a bowl of lemons, a wedge of Brie,
a pitcher of red wine, a cut-glass vase
filled with orange and yellow sweetly-
budding mums. *Natures morte.*
It may as well be a morgue
housed in the hospital basement
with its creased paper sheet
draped across a stainless steel table
where a fresh corpse has been
laid out with his rosy head,
sponged genitals, fatty,
waxen thighs, a tuck of string
around his tagged big toe.
The isolated, objectified body.
As long as I live I will never love
the polite lines and dead air
framing those lavish portraits of fruit,
the thickly-painted plates and glasses,
that grotesque whiff of flowers.

Francine Sterle

Second Sight

1
Found stunned northside of Townline Road,
the snowy owl drove boxed in my car
two hours to reach the raptor volunteer
who held the half-blind bird overnight
then rode four more hours before
delivering it, disoriented,
to a steel table where men
took a silver scalpel to its head.

2
In my cupped hand, the real
fruit of Eden: smooth, leathery,
thick-skinned, forbidden for its
crimson juice, thin vesicles,
dripping pulp. The venous-
colored seed Persephone welcomed
into her mouth. It was the owl
perched at the threshold of Hell
who saw her swallow, who
denounced her for obediently
swallowing. It was the owl.

3
A deep sweetness on the tongue.
The simple *yes* I give
to the things I love.

4
Thrashing in the closed
coffin of that box, the owl punched
holes in old cardboard where
the hooked beak broke through.
Specks of blood and battered feathers
littered the makeshift nest.
No matter the effort,
wings failed to bring it to flight.

Francine Sterle

5
Over the pitched spine of an abandoned barn,
a ghostly owl, over
snow rows and fence posts,
over chips of bottle glass flashing
in a ditch and the deserted
undiminished miles,
over the emotional weight of that road,
it crosses straight out in front of me,
and the car so accurate as it skids
on ice, slides trunk-first into a tree.

6
Where the moon has been shining,
a predatory eye
and something breathing
beyond the gate where the cemetery lies.

7
Like pond lilies floating open,
unspoiled feathers
drape my gloved hand,
but I feel claws leafing out,
gripping me, not wanting to let go.
Behold the convulsive dive,
the heartstopping drop as it breaks
a crust of snow to take exactly what it wants.

8
A savage, unlucky creature,
the Chinese say, terrifying
because it devours the mother.
Yet how do you judge one
that eats what it sees,
sees what it eats?

9
The moon: no light of its own—
it is all reflection.

Francine Sterle

10
Those milky wings hunt me
into the night as if I were harmless
as a field mouse or tree frog
offering nothing
but a penny of consciousness
as it dies. My eyes close.
I whirl down,
a tide of bones at my feet.

11
One eye changes places
with another. The owl swivels its neck,
sees me with one good eye. A moon appears,
and I float there, my reflection
gliding in icy light. There I am
fully seen for the first time.
There I am, fingers brushing its neck—
out of foolishness or arrogance
or grace—stroking it as I would
a lover's brow, touching my lips
to the dangerous pillow of its head.

Entering the Landscape

1
A tree adapts to a position.
Dropped on a rock, the chance seed
steals nourishment where it can—
a lip of water, some flowerless moss.
Roots slender as spiders' legs
grip with a bold tenacious hold
the stone's uneven surface,
push down into a hairline crevice,
push deeper and deeper, not stopping
until they touch the transforming soil.

2
No more liberated seeds
or winged, crimson-tinted fruit.
What's planted grows. The soil
sends up its fixed idea,
shapes it into a shoot, a branch,
a bud. When a leaf appears
limp and edgeless or sharply
toothed or deeply fluted as a
fish's fin, it's easy to forget
the time spent packed in the bud,
folded there like a fan or rolled to fit
the tiny dome from which it rose.

3
Just as dawn flees the rising sun,
disappearing a split second before
he reaches her, Daphne
metamorphosed right there
on a riverbank, earth and water
joining forces so the laurel could thrive.
When a sighing wind lifts beneath her,
the green skirt sways, the mythic limbs
rising and falling as a lover's might
inside the beloved's welcoming arms.

Francine Sterle

4
What a torturous shape for a tree:
a straying crown, flimsy foliage,
the rugged homeliness of the bark,
a leggy trunk artless as a pencil,
the scanty, unbalanced branches.
A large snapped bough dangles
downhill over an eroded bank.
Low sun lights the pendent branch
where hoarfrost has collected.
How clumsy it looks under its burden;
how cold against the snow-charged sky.
Its isolation attracts attention
the way a misshapen bush atop
a barren hilltop becomes a landmark.
No question where the eye will come to rest.
Though not as pleasing as the downy-coated
poplar, the polished holly, I've been given
this tree to plant in the soil of the page.

5
Birdsong spreads through the boughs.
Music that never stops arriving.

6
Seen against moonlight,
trees lose their detail.
Only the shape is unique,
conforming to the habit of the tree.
From a distance, it's easy to distinguish
a balsam fir from a white spruce
even as blue panoramic shadows
fill every hollow between them,
tier upon tier disappearing in the dusk.

7
There is an uncertain territory
between night and day.
An unexpected clearing opens
among dreaming trees.

Francine Sterle

Those you love will be
everywhere you look:
the parent bough and its straying
offshoots, an aging elm log,
ready for firewood, breaking
into blossom, the just
record of time and stress
seen in that gaunt skeleton
ready to defy another
century of storms.
We withdraw into ourselves,
taking the world with us,
inventing, all over again,
the circumference of our lives.

8
After an exquisite gray
washes over wintry trees
and familiarity fades,
dropping its leaves; after
shadows fall without distinction
and the road blurs into the bank,
the bank into the thicket; after
the cadence of falling snow,
the melting sunlight; after the resinous
sweetness of a forest, the habitual
wind, the theatrical landscape;
after the solitude, the harsh
solitude; after the inwardness,
the exile to the wooded slope;
after the vitality of the stalk,
the suave lines of a bussing twig;
after the subtle undulations of a stem
and the graceful rhythm of a branch
and the dance, the dance
you must enter to understand,
my words crop the underwood
and sky breaks through tilting leaves
and the very quality of air is a poem.

Francine Sterle

Prayer

Because it is the cloth of grief
Because it covers us with light
    as if it were a garment
Because the threads of it make a bridge
      across temptation
Because its robe is woven into every mother's cry
Because it allows a daughter to wear
      hope's colors in her hair
Because it swaddles us as a blanket swaddles a baby
Because it protects us
Because it binds faith to affliction
Because it knows we are frail
    and its mercy cloaks us
Because it is the braid of fear
    the ribbons of thanksgiving
Because it is a precious lace we make
    with our neediness and longing
Because belief need not precede it
Because doubt will not diminish it
Because it is the green shawl of the forest
    the delicate gown of a flower
Because it teaches us to love the world
    teaches us wonder
    teaches us reverence
Because it opens the seam of the heart
    and ties us to the divine

Teach me to wear your grace like a coat
Teach me to quiet my thoughts and speak
Teach me to silence my words and listen

Francine Sterle

Whenever I write, I am aware of how difficult it is to reconcile the world beyond the poem with the self-conscious act of putting words down on paper. Because I am introspective by nature, the dynamics that guide my creative process are intuitive, emotive and associative. In my work, I attempt to explore poetic strategies that allow full expression to private material—the parts that are beyond speech—by finding correspondences in the natural world to express and amplify that material. I am drawn to the compressed lyric which suppresses as much as possible what Eugenio Montale termed "the structural-rational cement." By cutting away some of the connective tissue of traditional narrative structure, I am forced to grapple with the inherent tension between sequential narrative and non-linear experience. Many of my poems have a prismatic quality and depend on an incremental progression of time and detail. My poems tend to rely on an attentiveness to nature. I am rooted in the landscape of northern Minnesota—its lakes and stunted pines, wildlife and wildflowers. I am not simply in this landscape but of it, having lived here most of my life. It is only natural, then, that when I sit down to write, this is the world that enters me. When I focus lyric attention on the world outside my window, what resonates is the savage, the sensual, the redemptive. When I speak of nature, I am also speaking of myself, in an attempt not to erase the boundaries between inner and outer but rather to harmonize the conscious and unconscious meanings that flow between the two.

Francine Sterle

Eugene McCarthy is well-known as the U.S. Senator from Minnesota who opposed the war in Vietnam and has run for the presidency as an alternative to party regulars. McCarthy grew up in Watkins, Minnesota, and attended St. John's University on his way to a political career that made him conspicuous as a highly respected critic of the American political system. While his writing has included several books about politics, few know his many other published works, which include children's stories, satire, and commentaries on the zen of baseball (he played baseball professionally for a time.) His most recent book in this vein is *An American Bestiary* (Lone Oak Press, 2000). Poetry has been a long-time passion. Lone Oak Press published his *Selected Poems* (1997) and is mounting an archive of his work on the world-wide web.

The Public Man

He walks, even in daylight, with arms outstretched.
Fish-like he shies at shadows,
His own, following him, nose to ground
Like a blind bloodhound.

Gray fish swim through
The cavities of his skull.
He feeds the sterile cows, the steers of no desire,
With the mast of the bitter grapes.

He closes his eyes to fireflies,
And his own light
Which once burned bright
Is yellow tallow.

His words rise, like water,
Twice used, from the cistern pump.
And then go out in a wavering line
As beagles run, intent on catching rabbits.

Like a gull, crying with tired voice,
He looks back, often, into the fog.
Each night he holds his head of stone between his hands,
As his elbows slowly sink through the tabletop.

Eugene McCarthy

Three Bad Signs

The first Bad Sign is this:
"Green River Ordinance Enforced Here.
Peddlers Not Allowed."

This is a clean, safe town.
No one can just come round
With ribbons and bright thread
    or new books to be read.
This is an established place.
We have accepted patterns in lace,
And ban itinerant vendors of new forms
    and whirls,
All things that turn the heads of girls.
We are not narrow, but we live with care.
Gypsies, hawkers and minstrels are right
    for a fair.
But transient peddlers, nuisances, we say
From Green River must be kept away.
Traveling preachers, actors with a play,
Can pass through, but may not stay.
Phoenicians, Jews, men of Venice—
Know that this is the home of Kiwanis.
All you who have been round the world
    to find
Beauty in small things: read our sign
And move on.

Eugene McCarthy

Grant Park, Chicago

Morning sun on the pale lake,
on plastic helmets, on August
leaves of elm, on grass,
on boys and girls in sleeping bags,
curled in question marks.

Asking
the answer to the question
of the song and of the guitar
to the question of the fountain,
of the bell and of the red balloon
to the question of the blue kite
of the flowers and of the girl's
brown hair in the wind.

There are no answers
in this park, said the captain
of the guard.

Then give us our questions
say the boys and girls.

The guitar is smashed,
the tongue gone from the bell,
all kites have fallen to the ground
or caught in trees,
and telephone wires
like St. Andrew, crucified,
hang upside down.
The balloons are broken
flowers faded in the night
fountains have been drained
no hair blows in the wind
no one sings.

Eugene McCarthy

Three men in the dawn
with hooks and spears,
three men
in olive drab gathered
all questions into burlap bags.
They are gone—

There are no questions
in this park
said the captain
of the guard.

There are only true facts
in this park
said the captain
of the guard.

Helen did not go to Troy.
The Red Sea never parted.
Leander wore water wings.
Roland did not blow his horn.
Leonidas fled the pass.
Robert McNamara reads Kafka
Kirkegaard and Yeats—and he said on April 20, 1966,
"The total number of tanks in Latin America is 974,
This is 60 percent as many as a single country,
Bulgaria, has."

There are only true facts
in this park
said the captain
of the guard.

Place of Promise

I hunt for the white doe
in winter dusk—snow
falling in the forest of birch
and of beech. I know
my search must end.
I am in the place of promise
with no track or trace.

Whiteness alone, not light
holds back the punctual night.
I have walked through spring
white against green,
of anemone, laurel and thorn,
searched the pale mist of plum,
put my hands in the tangled skein
of wild cherry.

In my passing, I scattered
the scant white of summer,
the wind-drift of willow and thistle.
My knees knew the white
of daisies and asters
that spin in the wind
in the fall.
I waded thigh deep
in the dry foam of milkweed.

Eugene McCarthy

Kilroy

Kilroy
the unknown soldier
who was the first to land
the last to leave,
with his own hand
has taken his good name
from all the walls
and toilet stalls.

Kilroy
whose name around the world
was like the flag unfurled
has run it down
and left Saigon
and the Mekong
without a hero or a song
and gone
absent without leave
from Vietnam.

Quiet Waters

There are quiet waters
where a berry dropped
by a bird flying
starts ripples that
from the center of the pond
spread in concentrics, dying
in silence at the feet of the blue reeds.
I now know where these waters are.

A woman once told me that I shouldn't be disturbed about not winning the presidency. You've written a poem about a mouse, she said, which is more important than that.

As a general rule, I believe that the artist should remain somewhat detached and independent of politics, but when the issues are as crucial as they were in 1968, no citizen, no matter what his vocation or profession may be, can remain completely aloof. It was a year in which artists had to be, as Albert Camus has said, both artists and men even to the point of being prepared to neglect their special work or calling in order to involve their person, their time, and their art in the country's problems. "If we intervene as men," wrote Camus, "that experience will have an effect upon our language. And if we are not artists in our language first of all, what sort of artists are we?"

Eugene J. McCarthy

(Photo by Paul Prefontaine)

Joan Wolf Prefontaine has spent most of her life in Minnesota. Born in St. Cloud, she grew up in Northfield where she eventually attended Carleton College. A long-time presence on the Minnesota literary scene, she has done much to encourage other writers while working her way to graduate degrees in both poetry and theology. In 1997 she and her husband Paul moved to a small lake south of Deerwood, Minnesota. From there she continues to nurture her work as teacher, editor, freelance writer, and book reviewer. She has published work in many journals, and several of her poems have been set to music by Minnesota composers and performed. A collection of her poetry, *The Divided Sphere* (written under Joan Wolf), was published by Floating Island Press of California.

Earth Tones

She had thought she had nothing
more to say, that words had dried up
in her like the valley streambed
after an interim of sparse rain.
Then she sat taking in the night's

long breath, hearing the frogs
below her in the marsh that was so bare
of water it could almost be called 'field,'
heard them chanting in unison the end
of summer, the glad, ponderous,

sonorous pre-burial songs of the leaf-
floating time. They never lifted
their voices skyward to emulate fog
or mist or light but simply persisted,
droning prayerfully like Buddhist

monks with no extraneous gestures
or courtesies, or like farmers tethered
to the old ways, humming closely
with root-rhythms and rocks
and the sleeping habits of seeds.

She was wrong. Darkness, not silence
was what had claimed her, and now
she must seek the low, communal
notations of the soil, the penetrating
resonances with which to explain this.

Joan Wolf Prefontaine

Raspberries

Shadows wade through
these brambly beds

where it is worth the rasp
for the flavor, worth

the July heat for
fingers' royal stains.

Black thimbles and red:
the sublime perennials

in this thicket, reveals
itself in compact drupelets

of its own sugary fullness.
And we are all seekers

here: bear's tongue,
finch's beak, hands

that will roll a buttery
crust for an after-dinner pie.

The earth, too, draws in
its generous portion

of sweetness as the choicest
release with a touch.

Joan Wolf Prefontaine

Choreography

Just over Waterford bridge, we snap
on our skis to gleam over white

slants and persuasions. Above,
a red-tailed hawk relaxes

into her hunger, ringing
the unabbreviated sky. Here

a cornfield bequeathed to coons
and crows, here an archway

of snow-needled pines. What
does it matter that the wind-chill

registers with some meteorologist
at thirty-five below? Today

everyone presses the path rosy
with hellos, silky ski costumes

swishing like grace notes through
impartial blue stanzas, poles

plumbing profane silences
like the pencils of marathon writers,

and while for a few, it has been
given, to glide more swiftly

or artfully than the rest toward
the page's red margin at dusk,

should that be appraised, ultimately,
as anything of remarkable

worth under the inconclusive
memoranda of the stars?

Joan Wolf Prefontaine

Early Planting

(For my father)

The man leans on his rusty hoe,
pockets crammed with seed
for the early planting:
broccoli, beets, peas, lettuce,
whatever might tolerate frost,
and laughs at the hungry boy
who steps out of him again.
He laughs and the boy laughs
and they stand together in the dirt
under the erratic April clouds.

The man thinks: this boy comes
and goes like a flicker from his hole.
Suddenly cold, the man turns his back
to the wind which blows in gusts
off Turtle Bay tipping the furry grass.
When he glances up, the face
more familiar than his own is gone.

The man hoes and plants his seed
all the while singing—or is it
the boy's voice—the lullaby
he once sang to his children:
"Over the rolling waters go,
Come from the dying moon and blow,
Blow him again to me, While my
little one, While my pretty one sleeps."

Flying over the house from the lake
where the last ice-beads
have recently melted away,
a loon laughs—his strange,
hysterical almost-human laugh.

The man rests, leans his hoe
against winter's ragged edge,
thinking about boy, loon, ice,
how all apparent solids
diffuse and begin to flow.

Joan Wolf Prefontaine

Tornado Salad

While a column of air gained force in the west
with its funnel-shaped extension of a cumulonimbus cloud,
we brought the sailboat in, two sisters, wondering at the eerie calm,
catching the last windflaws under the grey-green wall of sky.

> Years ago my great-grandmother and her storm-dreading sister stood
> at the high living room window above the same lake brooding,
> anticipating on hot humid afternoons just such a storm as this,
> women laced with premonitions, from one generation to another.

First the hail came, noisy as woodpeckers on a metal plate,
wild syncopations on the stepladder and aluminum fishing boat,
the excitement of selecting ice stones "almost as big as golf balls"
to stock the freezer for later proof that we at last were here.

> Before the storm I had dreamt of whirlwinds for weeks,
> of diving into drainage ditches, hugging the muddy earth,
> of falling face first into cornfields, the cyclone at my back
> and I woke to blame my forebears for cowering at portentous weather.

But you, sister, were nearly fearless, chopping tomatoes and scallions
like a skilled surgeon with a deadline, adding garbanzos, parsley,
    cucumbers
in a dressing of sour cream, and the salad sat ready in its green bowl
    above us
as we huddled, tense and attentive to the sound of freight trains,
    among roots.

> Not to worry then, there will always be storms and hunger
> and if we are lucky, a tornado salad made by someone we love
> after we've stepped up from the darkness to measure out our worth,
> after we've endured together whatever danger will pass.

Joan Wolf Prefontaine

Why I Pity the Woman Who Never Spills

For she misses the luxury of dribbling
marinara sauce on white silk,

of merlot falling at uproarious dinner
parties onto beige lace tablecloths,

picnics where mustard, baked beans,
toasted marshmallows and melted

chocolate all leave their winsome,
gregarious stains on Levis and lips.

For she misses the thrill and mess of it all:
hands infatuated with bread dough,

logic blemished all day with sly innuendoes
and double entendres, the child in the lap

with the histrionic green lime popsicle kiss,
the kettle with its secret military spices

longing in its heart of heart to spill the beans,
mangoes eaten au natural in bathtubs,

sweet-talking, profane juices softening
the millstones and milestones of the body,

the plum's intemperate noddings in a neighbor's
nonchalant field, tartness oozing like ink

across obeisant fingers, strawberries,
caught red-handed in golden-straw beds,

falling upwards towards one's mouth—
small, fierce advocates of sumptuous rendezvous.

I say to her: Spill, Spurt, Squirt, Splash, Splatter,
Spot, Spree, Sprinkle, Dribble, Drabble, Oozle,

Offend, Transcend, Transude, Transgress, Transpire,
Perspire, Percolate, Partake, Propagate, Create!

Joan Wolf Prefontaine

***My poetry has always been strongly influenced by Minnesota's seasons and landscapes**—by the woods, prairies and fields of the southeastern part of the state where I spent most of my life, and by the lake country two hours north of the Twin Cities where I now reside (and where I used to be a summer resident). I have done a fair amount of traveling, but even while visiting distant places, I have found myself more likely to write poems set in my home state. It is a feeling not unlike that of being haunted, I guess—of being unable to let go of certain atmospheric qualities and specters from the past. I am continually transformed by the natural world which surrounded me as a child and by a number of the people who resided there as well. Often I write a poem many years after the experience it describes has occurred.*

As much as I have grown to enjoy using the computer for research and assorted correspondence, I, like many other poets, write my first drafts with pen and paper. Only in the final editing process am I able to work with words on a screen. For me, poetry seems to require connection to the actual physical world. It is as if the pen in my hand were a walking stick, helping me navigate the empty, snowy landscape of the page. If all goes well, my walking fills the blankness in with memorable lines and characters.

The trick, it seems, is to be able to write through any weather—fog so thick the ice houses on the lake cannot be seen, ice storms that take down power lines and leave you stranded for days, Indian summer warmth when there is nowhere else you would rather be but home. I once heard a neighbor remark, "We don't need emotions in Minnesota. We've got weather!" But I think that when Minnesotans talk obsessively about the weather we are trying, in our peculiarly reticent way, to describe the passionate uncertainty of our carefully concealed lives.

Joan Wolf Prefontaine

(Photo by Ann Kolden)

James Togeas, who has published only a handful of poems during a writing life that spans several decades, is original for his desire to integrate his knowledge of chemistry, science history, and cosmology into the sonnet and other traditional forms. An Iowa native, he earned his degrees at St. Olaf College, the University of Minnesota and the University of Iowa. Currently he is Professor of Chemistry at the University of Minnesota-Morris. In addition to essays on atoms and elements, he has written short fiction and four unpublished novels.

Austerity

She ruffed her wings who barred me at the door
        Behind which rumor threw a splendid feast.
Meager fare she gave who dared to give no more
        To slake a random thirst or break a fast.

She guards the place that's called Prosperity,
        Where what's not forbidden may be acquired,
But my passport's stamped Austerity,
        Where all's forbidden that's not required.

There I've the world in view from pole to pole,
        Fixed between God's finger and Nature's thumb,
A place where tough ideas ease the soul
        And words trimmed like sails are its equilibrium,

While behind the door flicker love and flesh
Like the wow and was of a lightning flash.

Scripts

Wind-driven flakes beat a rhythm on my skin
        As the air recites its blank hexameters of snow,
        But the storm's chant is in a tongue I do not know
And the poetry of storm in a meter I cannot scan.

Who will read the river as a hieroglyph,
        An illuminated letter on the manuscript of dawn,
        As ideogram what wind has chiseled in the cliff,
All in an alphabet from which no words are drawn?

The world's a book, a butterfly's a poem on a page
        We try to read, but with conviction in the bone
        Of a depth we cannot sound, a drift we cannot gauge,
Of text and context and quiddity, and no Rosetta Stone.

James Togeas

September Fog

When September conjures the fog's soft suffusion
    And autumn unsleeves silence for the beleaguered ear,
    And the heart, tired nestling, tries the magic air
(Our inner eye assured despite the outer's confusion),

Then let the apathetic hear the sniveler complain,
    The querulous rant when the garrulous fall still
    And the obstinate crack on an intransigent will
(Our inner realm as rich as the outer is inane).

Prodigal summer died destitute of private hours,
    But now the fog provisions beggared countrysides,
Provides for towns, embraces sun-bedazzled heirs,
    Encloses and excludes, pervades, softens, muffles, hides.

A tree; a shadowed nest; boughs hanging low;
Twilight; twig clusters; drops dangling in a row.

James Togeas

Angel of Belief

Each Easter we the death-indentured dream
The creak of stair and hinge at predawn murk,
Hear the door-latch catch, bleak in grief
The Marys gone with spice to the garden tomb,
This time to find the radiant angel of belief
Lordly there, dream to hear them running back.

Each Easter we the death-indentured start
And stare at the heart's dark, the dream's end lost;
Taste the host, dry as a coin on the tongue;
And turning in the dark press ear to stone
    To hear the Angel flutter past.

Comet

The comet dances with the sun: its orbit's curled
    In conic sections in our heads. It beguiles
Ten billion eyes fanned across a peacock world
    When it fans its tail across ten million miles.
Then, perihelion past, bends to its outbound pace
    Beyond the Dame of Love and Lord of War
And Paradise to let towards open space—
    The earth gone now and sun shrunk to star.
There titanic galaxies redden and recede
    Like trans-cosmic steamers plunging into night,
    And you're left adrift on the Sea of Naught,
Until "Let there be light" seems to have gone unsaid,
    And God's forgot His great decree
    That Being is but Nothing cannot be.

James Togeas

Empedocles

Elements are *rhizomata*, roots of things,
    That twine and segregate to the same twin
    Forces, Love and Strife, that underpin
All human blossomings and ravenings.

His thought has twists tongue-twistingly odd:
    Ontogeny recapitulates cosmogony;
    Embryonic growth and cosmic history
Spring alike from sphere-like forms of egg and God.

And so he said, it's said, *Sphairos* first gave birth
    To sphere-like trees when Strife perturbed its dream.
    For me, when trees are bare, their branches seem
Like bronchioles of pneumatic Earth,

    And I might ramify 'mid rhizomes there
    Were I exhaled, that is, if I were air.

James Togeas

Pick up an anthology and it's evident that the range of stuff called poetry is huge. That's fine. Homogeneity is dull.

I write verse. I hope it's also poetry. I suspect that I look farther into the past for exemplars than most contemporary poets. Most probably would find me out of step with the times, given my preoccupation with the sonnet form. But the sonnet challenges me in ways other poetic forms do not. Its compactness is what bedevils its creator. It ought to turn with the power of a syllogism, but have that power enhanced by sound and image; its logic should be both "head-logic" and "heart-logic."

In *Walden* Thoreau says that he writes in the first person because, "I am confined to this theme by the narrowness of my experience." We are finite creatures and inevitably our range of expression is limited by our finitude. It is a self that writes a poem: a poem is an expression of self. Hopkins likens all of our actions to the tolling of a bell:

"Selves—*goes itself*: *myself* it speaks and spells;

Crying What I do is me: for that I came."

However, in the best poetry the self is a point of departure. The events of our lives should be something which we transform into poetry rather than simply report. A tricky thing about writing a sonnet is finding content compatible with form. In principle the subject could be too little or too big for the fourteen lines. In my practice the latter is the problem, that the sonnet swells with a subject larger than the self and threatens to burst.

My hope is for a confluence of form and content, meaning that the subject, rhythm, and sound meld into a unity. There is no point in talking about perfection since there are no objective criteria for it. Instead I strive to produce a poem that pleases the mind with coherent thought, that's faithful to the heart, and satisfies both ear and eye.

James Jogeas

(Photo by Judith Connor)

Linda Back McKay lives with her husband—and their motorcycle—in Minneapolis. The recipient of several awards, she has published her poetry in a wide variety of literary publications. Her nonfiction book, *Shadow Mothers: Stories of Adoption and Reunion* (1998), and the recent Great American History Theatre production of *Watermelon Hill* were both based in part on her experiences, and those of other unmarried mothers who placed their babies for adoption in the 1960's. To complement her "day job" as an independent commercial writer and creative director, McKay conducts creativity and poetry writing workshops at cafes and bookstores. Her creative nonfiction, *Iron Horse Cowgirls,* and a poetry collection, *Ride That Full Tilt Boogie,* are forthcoming.

Ritual Branch

(After the photograph by Minor White)

All the years of wondering lost,
all the wonder of finding my son, fading
with that same loss and the small
part of him I am allowed. That,
and time, if time is kind,
to correct the memory.
My mother says, *Isn't it good
how things have turned out?*

That oak tree in our back yard
was mine, yet it held its own
life secretly. It was there, though,
and I could talk to it and be with it.
My mother needs to believe things
are good or else she would have to
find something else to believe.

I remember the shades drawn,
the accusations, the theft of my
integrity, the *how could you do this
to us*, when truth was it had been done to me,
their little bird, unable to flee or think.

Every mother should say, *You are not evil.
You are the heart of an oak tree, my love.*
I have seen to it that all my children
know they are not evil. But do they know
my love? My heart? Is this lesson
being corrected for my benefit?
Distance corrects the memory with a soft
blow to the midsection. Tonight
we will burn the ritual branch, flame
against lake, frost on the window melting.

Linda Back McKay

Night Measures

(For Fran)

May it happen when you least expect it.
You'll be lying on your bed with all your emptiness
on top of you. Nothing will happen until time
is ready to let you up. You'll be lying there,
looking just like your mother, little gray bird,
with your own mute package of regrets.
None of us wants to know what's going on inside
our craft of bones, propelled network of instinct.
The hummingbird hovers faithfully in selfish blossoms.
An owl is pursued by crows mourning their foolish eggs.
But listen. When night
measures your unobtrusive song,
the pile of clothes at the foot of your bed will take shape
and the coat on the hook will remember your arms.
We own our own flesh, I suppose,
so when the earth melts under the sky as it is right now,
and the electric hum of cicadas suggests endless flight,
I want you to believe in birds and ask,
whatever soared from me once?

Linda Back McKay

Indian Cemetery

From crooked gate, hewn steps, the hill memorial
holds the names of souls who have left their bodies
here: Joe Beargrease. Mrs. Blacklock.
Mary Newfeather. Baby This and Baby That.
Having been sent home in the middle of things,
they are folded into their mother,
where they can listen for eagle drums
at the pow-wow grounds across the street.

At the café, we study our bottomless
cups of coffee, as if we could see
through the telescope of history.
We are so happy, you say. *We
are so lucky*. We do not speak of
the nervous river, nor any law.

We all return to our leafy places, where we were
greened, knee-high in volunteers from
an earlier planting.

We browse the raspberries,
ponder acorns.

Let us not think so little of spring
when we climb that hill again, but watch
each point of how the sumac turns
and the survivors survive.

Linda Back McKay

Dislocated Worker Project
Fairmont, Minnesota

When the men come home with the news, the women count
bags of peas in the deep freeze, though the International
Brotherhood of Teamsters has promised to help.
Over their grim beers, imposing heads of opposing horses
on the backs of their jackets, the men finger the paperwork from Local 154.
They can smell the rotting file folders at the Great Union Office in the Sky
where the big bosses meet in a flurry of indifference.
The head honcho wears a pinstripe suit and Buddy Holly glasses.
He won't be counting his bags of frozen peas.
He only feeds fresh to his family, lean beef and couscous,
as potatoes are gauche and rice is for chinamen.
The women at home draw the blinds and turn on all the lights.
They call each other on the phone. They pass fear back and forth
like a football. Their arms are muscled, having loved
the blue earth even in winter white-outs
when fathoming the road ahead
is impossible. The moon is pale as a dead fish. The women gather
their aprons and knead the dough of their wombs while the men ride pickups
with rifles under the seats. There is a sound of waiting, an animal sound.

Responsibility

In the garden with five mosquitoes per inch,
I dance a hop slap set of steps and squat plant
to plant, helping their quality of life, hoping
for tomatoes. It is all so easy and joyful
if you think about it, being overfed and free
in America. You get rid of all the tacky
furniture and buy new. You hire the painter,
lilacs bloom, a good movie comes to video,
you sleep like the dead. The children who can't
go home again are stories in the newspaper
you want to cancel because it's all bad
news. You've raised your children.
Most of us are not pure. Every choice is a loss.
It's not my life that is difficult.
I know there is sorrow but there's nothing I can do.
Give a little money, volunteer for some things.
I'd go to church if I thought it would do any good.
It feels fresh here in the garden, washed by rain,
sunny again. The pepper plants are blooming.

Linda Back McKay

The Barn Poem on Highway 19

We are black leather riders,
safe as two eggs on a spoon.
Drops of rain blur the windshield.
My monkey arms and legs hold tight.
I am eyes and ears on two wheels.
My hair is blown out behind me,
a tail off our thundering steed.
We lean into the next turn.

The Barn Poem. Faded
block letters on the side of a barn,
composed by a pioneer giddy with the thrill of it.
Twenty years ago or so, he stood on scaffolding
to publish his ancestral worship:

> *... wind walks after the storm*
> *men step up from the ground*
> *with the world in their eyes*
> *and roll the harvest home ...*

A poem passes quickly on a motorcycle,
but lingers in my own breath.

> *... fire in the burning hive ...*

The oaks have been careful to hold their leaves,
but things have a life, and things
happen, like secrets in the bluff country
and the incongruous ghosts we chase.

Linda Back McKay

Creating a poem requires courage and faith*—courage to begin the process and faith to allow the poem to become what it needs to be. When I'm in a new poem, there is almost always a point where the poem starts to take over and explore its own directions. That is when I know it's probably going to be good, and that's when I know I must move over, in a way, and let the poem direct the process.*

As writers, we all start with the same dauntingly blank page. Every poem begins with fear, its initial energy. It is only after I relax with the fear that I am able to bring forth a poem. Many of my poems are born on motorcycle rides, which is like flying and fear of flying at the same time. I love the purr of the engine, the scent of late August, a ribbon of Minnesota road, the flash of a deer, the dance of pure freedom. Riding always reminds me of life. It brings me closer to myself and the universe that cradles us all. I want to experience every moment of what passes before me. I want to ride—and write—to live. And keep the rubber side down.

Linda Back McKay

(Photo by Connie Bickman)

Richard Broderick developed an intense commitment to poetry while supporting himself as a freelance writer. His essays, columns and articles have appeared in both national and regional journals, and his short fiction was collected in *Night Sale* (New Rivers Press, 1982). The winner of awards for both his investigative reporting and for his creative writing, he has had many poems published in prestigious literary magazines. *Woman Lake* (New Rivers Press, 2000) is his first collection of poems. He also co-edits *Great River Review* while living in St. Paul.

Equinox

*(On September 23, 1991, the full moon coincided
with the autumn equinox for the first time in 29 years.)*

The sun sails past the equator tonight,
heading for its berth on Antarctica's
icy barb, dragging with it the blue stone
ballast, this once-in-thirty-years full moon.

Daughter, we stand in the wake of passage,
your small face shadowed by the coraled spruce
building itself up past the rooftops
to untroubled sky. It's calm at these depths;

the yard rolls away in quiet abeyance.
When next, if ever, we stand together
to witness this rare conjunction, your hand
will not fit so snugly in my own

and will have been shaped in subtle ways
by the memory of another's hand.
But for now, at this silent turning
of the autumnal tide, no strong current

pushes us backward or forward through time.
There is only the deep, abiding groundswell
bearing us along, and our nighttime rhymes
about the moon counting us to the house.

Richard Broderick

The Mountains of Florida

(After Wallace Stevens)

The mountains at the end of the mind
rise nowhere but on an old map of Florida,
drawn there to represent the limits of the known world
beyond which you may travel no farther,

unless it is to check into the yellow hotel by the harbor
whose only air-conditioning is the breeze
blowing sluggishly off the Indian river
and where, lulled by the ticking of palm trees,

you lie in bed and watch a motionless gecko
as the sweat trickles down your side
and joins the vapors of a breathless afternoon.
No more does the ocean sink its footings

into the bottom of the absolute, finding there,
instead, a false bottom, beyond which
lies another ocean, then another bottom.
Only these imaginary mountains, appearing

so irresolute among the cratered clouds at sunset,
will be there reliably, along with the gecko,
to meet all yearnings for the absolute,
tomorrow and tomorrow and tomorrow.

Richard Broderick

Moonrise over Lake Michigan

There must be a word for it,
this slow roll of the grooved ball bearing
as it rises in its slot, this intricate
mechanism of the earth turning
within the celestial clock.
And there must be a word for it,
this gathering of a gilded tide within us,
the heart ascending and going forth
to meet the molten spill rushing
toward us over the black waters,
the swell flashing as it lifts.
And there must be a word for it,
or at least should be a word for it,
the tongue locked against the teeth just so,
the triggering click and release of breath
like a wave breaking, a word
that is the word for it and for the feeling itself,
just as there should be a word
for these moments when we turn
toward each other, faces shining, the same
thought forming between us.
Should be a word, but there is none,
unless it is the word the voice out there
keeps whispering again and again.
And so we sit and watch the moon
climb the sky and listen to the low surf
work the grain of sand under its tongue,
as if some day there might issue forth
a pearl, an opalescent, perfectly round
and smooth, perfectly apt word for it all.

Richard Broderick

After Reading the Unabomber Manifesto

I know the kind of hut he hid out in,
the heaps of paper yellowing
like rotten snow beneath freckled
windows, the pages of magazines
and books nestled by the wind's
forefinger, up a rocky draw
where the pine boughs swish
like beaded curtains, the silence outside
a physical presence, the air at noon
baking in the reflected heat
of black scree sprawling downslope,
a solitary Camp Jay preening and
screeching on a lower branch,
and always the dryness, cracking
the mouth from the inside out,
tongue whiskery, the lips looking branded
as if by smoldering words held too long.
And no relief in the distances,
no dust of someone approaching
with a cry of love, no news
of a reprieve. In that solitude, he
came at last to see the way they
put him together, intricate mechanism
hair-triggered to explode like a fireweed
releasing its seed to the flames.
But there was no fire here, nothing
but the slow combustion of being
alone all the time, day and night.
And so, from the parts of himself,
he re-configured his packages,
wrapped in plain brown paper to signify
simplicity, and dispatched them
to places beyond the thunder,
messages from a new Thoreau.

Richard Broderick

On Moss

Blessèd be the moss that beards the face
of exposed embankments deep in the forest,

that spreads its feathery caul over old stones,
breaking them down, starting them on their way

from loneliness toward the community of soil.
And blessèd be the moss that lays its carpet across

the north-facing toes of white birch trees, showing
the direction down paths where it will never go.

And blessèd be the moss that comforts
the torn hoof of the starving doe in winter,

and that waits patiently, even beneath
ice-crusted, knee-deep late January snow,

to keep for us, who might otherwise despair,
the jewel-green promise of our renewal.

Sundays Spent Working at Home

It always makes me feel so virtuous,
as if this were not my own, but God's house,
the words on the page falling bright and dense,
the snow outside a rite of innocence

renewed. Holy this hour. Holy the groan
of wind and walls, the child's voice in the next room,
the walk we'll take a little later with the dog
beside the river and around the bog.

And holy the still-later, winding-down time
with a book in the bath, a glass of wine
and a mind that continues to spark
long after I lie down and pray to the dark.

Richard Broderick

Swimming Laps

I swim an hour as if to chase the boy
I was, drowning, drowned,

beneath the closing waters
of the past, the boy who splashed

all day down by the beach, who could
hold his breath until his father,

watching, reached the point of panic.
Now, breathless, my father lies

at depths beyond the gasp of fear,
while in the pool, just past a mile

earned lap by lap, I seem to slip
inside another skin in which

the boy I was and the man I am
swim toward each other, breathing

easily now side-by-side, afloat
in memory, our native element.

Richard Broderick

In a letter Emily Dickenson once explained *that she wrote to hold "the Awe" at bay, meaning, in her special lexicon, a response to life so intense that at times it threatened to sweep her away.*

For most writers the writing life probably begins with a confused impulse to assert oneself through personal expression. But over time, if we're lucky, if we stick to it, this impulse may evolve into a kind of spiritual discipline by which we learn to steady ourselves before the work, and thus before the world. Maybe that's why writing attracts the devotion of so many unsteady people. When I compose a good poem I compose myself as well.

Over the years I've learned that it's possible to create a life for yourself through writing, a way of seeing and thinking and living in the world while not being absorbed or annihilated by it. Through poetry I have come to possess new eyes and new ears, as if the poetry has produced a subtle alteration in my brain patterns. I am so much more attentive than I used to be, so much more eager and able to be quiet, as if I'm on an inward-bound journey away from noisy distractions, all the getting and spending of our powers.

How this process takes place is, of course, a mystery. Like life, like death, it is both utterly fathomless and commonplace as breathing. I am merely grateful that long ago I chose a path that, over time, has allowed me to hold the Awe at bay.

(Photo by Sasha Barnes)

Debra Cooke Barnes spent eleven years as a civil engineer designing bridges and highways in Colorado and Minnesota. Finding it challenging to raise four children, juggle work, and still keep her sanity, and needing a new creative outlet, she took up poetry writing. Her training may help explain why she prefers highly structured poetry. She finds that it takes months, even years, to fine-tune a sonnet. She has published some of her poems in literary journals, and was recently a finalist for the 1999 Howard Nemerov Sonnet Award as well as nominee for two Pushcart Prizes. Over the past four years, she has served as proofreader and assistant editor of Minnesota's *ArtWord Quarterly*.

There's Talk

While paused along a quiet city street,
I've held a conversation with a tree
And never felt the overwhelming need
To recognize it as soliloquy;
To hear the chatter of a cold cascade
I've walked a mountain mile in rain or shine
And, leaning on the mossy balustrade,
Felt no reproof for failing to join in;
But, left to my own devices in a room
Where disembodied voices rise, exhume
Discarded loves, ungrateful children, while
The pain's disguised with cocktails and a smile,
I take for mine the droning reprimand:
Solitude's fine. It's feeling alone I can't stand.

The World Has Turned

The world has turned to Autumn overnight.
Where lately, Summer's dust rose underfoot
And coneflowers nodded, dizzy in the bright
September sun, all's gone to berry and nut.
Today the leaves dance, golden and confused,
With wandering winds that speak a tripping tongue
And bustle into corners, well amused
To hint of frost and barrenness to come.
Enchanted by this garb of Nature's weaving,
The months have yielded leaf, sweet flower and vine;
But, ruddy with the fruit of Summer's leaving,
Autumn has abandoned Spring's design.
Three seasons' toil, from sun to setting sun,
It takes to mend what Winter rends in one.

Debra Cooke Barnes

Out of Time

Gone are the gentle days of Time's slow course:
From dawn to dawn, by simple show of hands,
A universal order was endorsed
As an hourglass honors gravity with sand.
No planet sweeping in its state of grace
Made its rounds to greater compliment
Than those minions on that honest face
Marking minutes saved and hours spent.
How Time plies his novel protocol!
Now digital, each second blinks its span
And spews a crimson stain upon my wall.
I miss the measured pace that Time outran:
Caught short within this pulsing circuitry,
The future isn't what it used to be.

Sonnet to Ravenna

Ravenna, shorn of every tress, lies waste.
That virgin jewel of the Puget Sea,
Whom heaven called a sister and embraced,
Is cloistered under concrete's lock and key.
What kind of creature squanders paradise?
Untouched by miracles beyond his frame,
A blind man peddling candles for a price:
Ravenna's bloom is cordwood to his flame.
Slow helper Time avenges maidenhood,
Unsheathing old wit's sharp and final thrust,
That he who desecrates that pathless wood
Is doomed to sleep within her tomb as dust.
Ravenna's conqueror has watched her burn:
From ash he rises, only to return.

Author's note: Seattle's Ravenna, a private park of national renown, was praised as "an artist's paradise" and received over 10,000 visitors in 1902. The park's giant firs stretched as high as 400 feet and were named for famous persons, including President Theodore Roosevelt, who visited the park. The City of Seattle condemned Ravenna in 1911, claiming it as "the most valuable piece of property in Seattle." The trees were most likely cut for firewood; it is speculated that they were sold by the park director for private gain.

Debra Cooke Barnes

Marriage at 42 Below

We were awakened in the early hours
That frigid night. The moon shone full on snow.
Thermometers had plummeted so low
Their hearts broke. Still, that wasn't what had roused
Us from our restless sleep; what we had heard
Was the separation, board from nail,
Of a house in agony, a joint portrayal
Of twenty years of building stress transferred.
Unearthly bumps and cracking raked the air:
Then frosty silence. (Can the children hear?)
Dulled witnesses to winter's wretched cold,
We heard the trusses testify to strain;
We listened to the bearing walls complain
And lay there, simply willing them to hold.

The Transcendence of Poetry

We sing the tale of Roland in his blood
Who, winding duty's horn, gave forth alarm
And, sanctified once more by crimson flood,
Preserved his liege lord Charlemagne from harm.
The bridal sonnet celebrates her grace;
A feast of springtide freshness! Every line,
Now paraphrased, engraves that lovely face:
No bitterer garnish than the lapse of time.
Of youthful words of beauty, Time takes measure;
He sifts the slag and ash of old laments.
Immortal are the lines we mortals treasure:
All poetry is grief in consequence.
We mold our monuments from smoldering embers:
Our transience is what the pen remembers.

Debra Cooke Barnes

Like most other poets, I was drawn to poetry early in life by a parent who read aloud to me. It wasn't until I was a parent that I rediscovered the joy of writing poetry, and I began to publish my work about three years ago. Writing is what I choose to do when I have a choice. There is no greater pleasure for me than to write a sonnet line that really works!

What makes good poetry enjoyable is that it is not generally self-absorptive, but begins with a thought that can be shared with someone else about something that is seen, felt, heard, touched, tasted, smelled, endured, remembered. By involving our own human observation and experience, and skillfully applying the rhythm and richness of language, we can make our work—and our joy in it—available to others.

Born of experience and skillfully crafted, poetry can be powerful stuff. How can we explain how certain words in combination touch us in ways we don't understand, bringing tears when we weren't particularly sad, or laughter when we weren't in a good mood to start with? Not only can poetry take the commonplace and make it noteworthy, it can take the extraordinary and put it within reach of every soul.

For me, writing a poem always begins with a view through a window—theoretical or literal—an observation made, an idea incubated, a phrase savored. Midway through the process, I begin to see the layers; the metaphor suggests itself through the selection of words that carry their own baggage. By the completion of the poem, which can take many months, the window has changed to a mirror, and the face that I see is my own.

"For a poet's work to be of consequence," says **Michael Kincaid**, "he must have not only studied the history of his art, but so incorporated it into his being as to make it his own history." Kincaid has made poetry a major part of his personal history since the late 1960's when he began publishing and reading his poetry and lectures. He has authored *To Walk in the Daylight* (1973), *Cave Light* (1985), *Inclemency's Tribe* (1990), an essay, *Orion's Return* (1992), *Vagrant Deity* (1999) and two other unpublished works. He lives in Minneapolis.

Northern Solstice

Summer is curing the robin of his impatience.
His musical insistence grown muffled among the leaves,
he is content to be the season's undertone.

The mulberry's purple fatness
has taken off his song's edge,
and parenthood has sobered him.

He has reached his northern limit,
the range of the sun's blessing,
and has no wish to go beyond.

But on the shortest night,
when the dormant light makes the horizon glow,
he rises to the pitch of his April madness
and competes with the overture of dawn.

(1975)

Hymn to Otherness

The glacier left no track in their mythology.
These rocks open heavens beyond ours.

Briars surround the stump where the ideal would sit down.
To step off the path makes the mind a hawk.

The bent bow suspends time.
The woods abound with immortalities.

Conjure the necessity of which you are the legend.
Fire is the science of ice.

(1999)

Michael Kincaid

Lunar Function

If the earth should die, the moon would be without a face, priestess of a grief beyond her power.

Moon: the light's ruined birthplace, flint from which it was struck, rock from which it hatched and flew.

Though spring is beyond the moon's imagining, new leaves defy the odds, the faith of opening buds a power of her devising.

The moon guards the empty sanctum maintained by superstition. The moon watches over the temple we live in, midwife to the Word.

Nature permits more than she forgives. The moon is the stamp of that license.

> Her light turns the mind into a wound. She is the flood dividing history, tidal wave that roars in dream silence.
>
> She fingers bare twigs with unspeakable tenderness.
>
> She incubates her negatives and nurtures a posterity oblivious of her sacrifice.
>
> Her nothingness is sworn to keep the secret of her magnitude. Despairing of the sun's kiss, her frost is the seed from which he grows.

>> Light needs a mirror
>> to conceive its own birth;
>> a mother to cry out,
>> a witness to go blind.
>>
>> Ruins of encounter,
>> our faces reinterpret
>> fatal certainties.
>> Our light belongs to earth.

(1985)

Michael Kincaid

Orion's Promise

Invisible by day,
transparent to the night,
only his outline shines.
He is the open gate for all that he pursues.

His emptiness disarms eclipse;
no face obstructs his view.

He traces both eternities.

His stride is the arc of chance,
track of the untried.

As the wolf's howl maps the night it spans,
his brilliance darkens earth.
His eye opens wilderness.

(1999)

Aeolian Oak

November is the year's bone,
sound of the irreducible,
song of the earth
uncontained by life's boundaries.
Autumn's broken gate
rattles in the wind of All Souls.
The sun gives ground.
The blown, deep-rooted stars
sing freedom to our bones.

(1988)

Michael Kincaid

Good Manners

Sheathe your lethal edge;
mute it in taciturn
oak bark;
disguise it
in the tiger's suavity,
the mountain lion's tact,
the flash
of the fox's escape.

Soften implacable
judgment
with the charity of thunder
and the earthquake's
harmlessness.

Shade your cruel eye
with night's infinity.

Wrap your deadliest thrust
in sunrise.

(1989)

The poem is language in the act of resuming its primordial nature, *renewing itself from the root, recovering root-meanings obscured and overlaid by usage. It is not, then, a* form *of language-usage, but the form of anti-usage, of communing with language at a depth usage may reflect in its abstractions—meridians of its two-dimensional map—but never reach.*

The root-meaning of a word is a destiny subsequent usages cannot escape: they must operate within *it; must honor it even in default, at the very height of their amnesia. This is the margin of the poet's art: he stalks himself and his readers with words made familiar by usage. The familiar is a camouflage for the poet's realignment of words with their primal destinies, his awakening of words from the sleep of usage to the fullness of their latent significance.*

The Indo-European root of the English word god *is* ghu-to-, *that which is called, called upon, invoked. A god, then, is a being that occasions speech, that which* calls *for utterance; indeed calls language into being. The sacred multiplicity of that call is reflected in the wealth of our vocabulary, occasions for the sacrament of language. The primal act of utterance affirms an ineluctable bond, human destiny given form in speech. Perpetuation of that bond is the destiny to which the poet is called.*

Michael Heffernan

(Photo by Joe Polski)

Norita Dittberner-Jax was born the sixth of seven children in Frogtown, a working class neighborhood of St. Paul. Her family was lively and musical. From her father she learned "the language of impassioned speech," and from her mother "its more playful elements." She came to writing through reading, but not until she was the mother of three in her early thirties. "I can't say why I had to do this difficult thing, carving out time, when it was so inconvenient." A collection of poems, *What They Always Were* (New Rivers Press), appeared in 1995. She has taught writing as an artist-in-the-schools, and now teaches at Johnson High School in St. Paul.

Sauerkraut Supper

(For Maryann Turner)

In honor of my birthday, you ask me
to the sauerkraut supper at St. Adalbert's
in Frogtown, my old neighborhood.

We meet in the church basement, line up
with the others, large men and women
who lack confusion about who
they are, who have lived by rules
of beer and coffee, who drinks it,
who pours it.

We are all happy to be here, moving
in line to the kitchen where the cook raises
the lid and steam rises like a genie.

She ladles the sauerkraut into great bowls;
other women pass us carrying platters
of roast pork, bowls of potatoes and
applesauce, baskets of bread, apple pie,
a feast of pale foods.

There isn't a green for miles, no broccoli,
no zucchini, those foreigners
in the new land, nothing sharp,
nothing to vex our souls that have traveled
so far from our starched childhoods,

as if we had all pushed our chairs back
from the table and vanished, years ago,
leaving our ghostly mothers
with the dishes.

Norita Dittberner-Jax

Levitating toward Duluth

I watch for the first pine, a flag of the country ahead,
and listen for the knock of geography shifting gears,
land rising out of bedrock and farm field.

Everything around me appears ordinary,
but inside I am waiting to be conducted
through something grand.

We climb higher, a long string of cars
crossing the St. Louis River, cutting through
the last elevation, then on to the top.

Suddenly the lake, huge and primal,
hidden behind the hunched shoulders of the hills
and with it the ships, bridges, and railroads,

all the commerce of water and land.
For a split second, we shimmer like trout
in the great flow of it, each bay and pier,

then shoot downhill into the stone channels
of the freeway, all our climbing released,
and arrive on the other side

of the city and onto the North Shore.
Quiet now, we are inside geography,
we hum along, a string of cars

whose passengers turn naturally
to the thin line between water and sky
where all our hopes gather.

Norita Dittberner-Jax

Love Letters

It is the quietest thing they've done
in years. Behind closed doors, on summer
afternoons, my daughters write letters
to young men. Paper disappears
from my desk; there is a run on stamps.
Fat letters to an airman apprentice
in Pensacola, pastel envelopes
to the drummer at music camp.

Slow summer afternoons of overcast skies
and deep humidity. My daughters in their
idleness watch soap operas and file
their nails while they wait for the mail,
the pattern of days so set, that when
my son hears from Rose in Honolulu,
after an absence of two years,
he asks for stamps.

Summer nights, my daughters fall asleep
to the strum of crickets and the whispers
of absent lovers. They waken, their faces
bright as peaches in the bowl of morning,
another day, another summer day, dozing
like cats in the sun, another promise,
write soon, write soon.

Norita Dittberner-Jax

Classroom

I wanted light to pour in
from the windows but the television
is mounted there, its cords tangled
like intestines.

I wanted curves,
the desks in half-moons, but the long train
of fluorescent light burns a hole
in the dark.

What I wanted was so grand,
I forgot the postcard of the gargoyle
I taped to the podium to absorb
any misery coming my way,
saying "Send them on up!"
your detentions, the trouble
at home, every bridge in your life
that comes up short,

feed them to the monster, let him
chew on it while you do
the mind's work of reading
and moving your hand across paper.

Senior English

Their heads are bent to paper, copying out
William Blake's "The Lamb" and "The Tiger"

on opposite sides of the notebook, adjoining
poems. They will graduate in three weeks and most

I will not see again, but here, now
we have the odd affection, the familiarity

and shyness of teacher and student, this closeness
over poems by mad William who lives on and on

becoming the gift I give these students
and the gift they give themselves.

Be accurate, I say, make them as beautiful
as you can; the room is very quiet.

In the courtyard the lilacs open.

West Seventh Street

This section of the city is dedicated
to repairs, used appliances,
rebuilt transmissions.
By-products of beer pour
from the smokestacks of the brewery.
At every corner its lineage is tacked:
Old Fort Road begat West Seventh.
The hooves of cattle beat
this ground. This street still
has the heart muscle of an ox.

The bus-driver knows it; see how he
turns the wheel with one finger?
This is his run more than the skyways
downtown unbuttressed by dirt.
He learned the blunt edge of the knife
here, the language of plumbers
who name their parts male and female
because one fits into the other.

Today he watches for spring four times,
twice uptown, twice downtown.
It squints off the bits of glass, rises
in a breeze off the river,
the river, so close
he forgets, living here,
that before the oxen
was the river
flicking its tongue at the land.

No one knows for certain where the name came from—Frogtown, *that part of St. Paul where I was born and raised. According to one theory, at one time the land was swampy and alive with frogs. According to another, it was named for the French who were the first settlers.*

I grew up surrounded by language, some of it foreign to me (German, Polish) but all of it expressive.

Writing poetry has been the great luxury of my life. As an urban high school teacher, I see every day how functional language is—and how critical. Writing poetry is a wonderful balance to that. I write about real things, and find the act of transforming experience and perception into poetry very satisfying. I run a kind of relay between worlds which keeps me refreshed.

In writing a poem, I try to get the words on the page to fit as closely as possible the picture I have in my head. I need lots of words to accomplish that, and I try them on until I get just the right ones. There's a click in my head and I can do no more. The whole process is a great joy to me.

Running through all this is the rich thread of music, the art in my family. My family always sang. My father was the church soloist and music is the ruling passion of a number of my siblings. When I began to write poetry, I felt I had broken new ground. Now I see that I have just changed the music.

(Photo by Doren Whitledge)

Born in St. Paul in 1957, **Jane Whitledge** grew up in Shoreview and attended the University of Minnesota for one year. In 1981 she moved to northern Minnesota and recently spent sixteen months living in a tent before moving to Duluth.

She's written poetry nearly all her life. At age fourteen her first published poems were featured in two national school magazines. The *Minneapolis Star & Tribune* covered this, with a headline that read: "Shy Poetess's Poem is Gone: 'Tears Made the Ink Run'"—her smiling face in the photo hardly tragic-stricken. The publicity was embarrassing but also encouraging; it went a long way in getting her to respect her audience, study poetry, read other poets and revise her work. She did not pursue publication until her mid-twenties, and has complemented her writing with widely published (and very funny) literary cartoons.

The Doll's Head

In a field burned over I found a doll's head
and put it in my pocket like an apple or a stone
and kept it there for days, my thumb probing
the open neck, my finger smoothing over a glass eye.

My winter coat, heavy and brown, seemed changed
by the head I carried, and it bothered me why
I picked it up and why I had to keep it.
But I kept it, because something now odd

about the coat made the coat and the cold alluring,
I thought, like a crazy-man's obsession; I held on
all that winter, amazed that no friend noticed
while I touched it there, secret broken head.

Jane Whitledge

Poet's Beginning

Only one rhyme
for *breath*: *death*,
& you're off
to a grave start.
Sorrow goes easy
with *tomorrow* as
pain insists on
rain. Add birds
because they *sing*
or *cry* and
open the way for
spring, & things
that *die*.
Or *sky*, with
its generous *blue*
and a thousand
possibilities
beginning with *true*,
with *you*. But
what happens when
grief, suddenly real,
summons *needle*,
not *leaf*, when
life's a mess
of *magazines*, *blankets*
and other rhyme-
less stuff?
You try *needle*;
you try *broken*;
you try again
till real birds rise
with real cries.

Jane Whitledge

Because My Father Worked Two Jobs

Because my father worked two jobs, we were rich,
I thought, had twice the money that others had:
There was more, there was less; I knew which was which.

I heard my mom brooding we'd end in the ditch
as she opened the mail that was always bad.
But daddy worked hard so I knew we were rich—

the way I loved a fat nickel, would always switch
any dime for that chunk, my math ironclad:
"Here is more, here is less, I know which is which."

Daddy said his boss was a son of a bitch.
I figured that boss was afraid of my dad
who worked two jobs and was twice as rich

and could rise while outside it was still pitch
dark. (Brief sleep subtracting what the day would add.)
There was more, there was less; he knew which was which.

When lots turned to little there appeared a glitch
in my logic: plain want, more vexing than sad—
because my father worked two jobs! We were rich!
There was more, then less; I learned which was which.

Jane Whitledge

Morel Mushrooms

Softly they come
thumbing up from
firm ground

protruding unharmed.
Easily crumbled
and yet

how they shouldered
the leaf and mold
aside, rising

unperturbed,
breathing obscurely,
still as stone.

By the slumping log,
by a dappled aspen,
they grow alone.

A dumb eloquence
seems their trade.
Like hooded monks

in a sacred wood
they say:
Tomorrow we are gone.

Jane Whitledge

Summer of Flowers

Sculling the canoe close to the granite outcrop
of an island, you show me the yellow cinquefoil
and tell me its pretty taxonomic name: *potentilla*.
A cluster of them is thriving in a cleft.
I note the small sticky blossoms, the minuscule
brilliance, the tidy leaves tucked close to rock.

It is the summer you are teaching me the flowers:
harebell, auralia, pale corydalis, trillium.
I summon their Latin names like mantras all through
the warm afternoons, pressing each new specimen
in your thumbed book: description, habitat, range
and season. Keepsakes of another ramble with you.

Where, my love, did you come from, bringing me knowledge
of the honeysuckle past my door? You with your woods
lore and St. Francis ease with nature, bringing me
to kneel beside the orchid, to taste the sweet nectar
of the columbine and drink the silky tea
of June's wild rose. What was the world before

you brought me the flowers? . . . Late spring
and all the leaves were darkening . . . a strange
bird was calling from a tree I could not mark
and it would not fly. It took me past the house
and set me on that path. Through black shade and
birdsong I went searching . . . Among sweet fern

and blueberry, I heard you call my name . . . Now
the warm seed splits, the green stem rises, and I,
my name new on your tongue, am all flower.
Pressed between your heart and the earth, I learn
the secret song of blossom, the root's soft fingerings,
and to your tender naming, I am all response.

Jane Whitledge

At the Wolf Kill

A dozen ravens scavenge
in a clearing among balsams
where a stain, like ignited tree-shade,
spreads a violent pink on the snow.
Dark wings rise at our approach
as ravens flee to a rim of pines
where they hunch, silhouettes
like so many hieroglyphs. One raven poses
on the far snow: dark ampersand
between us and the landscape.

We come to look, drawn by raven shrieks,
our snowshoes braiding a path through woods
to this place: remains of a deer, scraps
of hide, ribs; the head and spine intact
like some macabre hobbyhorse, the blank eye—
socket pleading indifference
to the slaughter.

Raven-tracks form a dense crosshatch that
cancels every wolf-print on the packet snow;
they etch a kind of cuneiform, an ancient
alphabet we'd find indecipherable if we tried.
We study the hard snow, faintly
looking for signs other than the obvious ones.
Wolves have already eaten most of the flesh.
Before leaving, we salvage the tongue.

Jane Whitledge

After I moved to northern Minnesota, my poems began *reflecting the natural world, while still being "about" the human: grief, mortality, love, struggle. My poetic voice, formerly confessional, became more detached and generalized—although I believe many of the nature-driven poems are alive because of a very personal investment in them. More recently, my poetry has shifted to a more straightforwardly human (for lack of a better term) verse, relying less on nature metaphor; the voice I've developed is more immediate and personal without, I hope, slipping into the confessional.*

I consider poetry my career, and for many years have set aside time daily for writing. I work in a variety of styles. I admire both free and formal verse; for me, it seems a poem chooses its own form—I rarely sit down with a fixed intention to write one way or another. In any case, I strongly believe that mechanics (not necessarily including rhyme and meter) enhance a poem's meaning when used skillfully.

I like poems that are surprising but also slightly uncomfortable, with emotions not commonly seen in poetry, such as embarrassment or shame—poems that challenge assumptions. Because I also work as a cartoonist—the process is not unlike creating poems—I'm at times drawn to humor in my poems as a means of making a point or dramatizing the absurd or darker side of things.

Jane Whitledge

(Photo by Eric Heukenshoven)

Steven Schild is "as Minnesotan as can be." Raised on a dairy farm outside Houston, Minnesota, he has lived in southeastern Minnesota ever since, with the exception of seven months in "another country called Waseca, a place trapped between prairie and hill country and not knowing what to do there." He has degrees from Minnesota universities, was married here, is raising a family here, and has buried his parents here. "Anything I know of this life I came to know in this land."

He has worked at construction, factory, journalism and public relations jobs. Currently he lives in Winona and teaches at St. Mary's University. His poetry has appeared in several literary journals including *ArtWord Quarterly*, *Touchstone*, and *The Wolf Head Quarterly*.

Beatitude: Cycle of Water

(For Corrine Arneson Schild)

These are the women who rise
before the sun in winter
to coax warmth
from cast-iron woodstoves
left untended all night.

These are the women who stand
over cauldrons of coffee,
the spattering fury of bacon,
the mad sizzle of red meat.

These are the women who reach
raw hands into roaring ovens,
rescue cakes, loaves of bread.

These are the women who hover
like dreams over feverish children,
bringers of blanket and damp cloth.

These are the women,
the women unseen,
invisible as vapor,
powerful as steam,
the women of men
once young
and consumed with fire.

Steven Schild

Sandwiches after the Service

Nothing like white bread and ham
to bring us back down to earth
after all those heavy organ notes
and bad singing and contemplation
of the great black beyond
and the great deal
the preacher says it is;

nothing like a steaming cup
of stout Lutheran coffee
to wash down all that dust-to-dust,
ashes-to-ashes that sounded so like
poetry in the version of King James
but seems a world away
in the paneled church basement
where old ladies
whose hands look like lefse
make sure that no table has an empty pot,
cut sponge cake so sweet
you can't turn it down,
worry whether there'll be enough

because a big crowd is starting to come in,
talking small talk with old friends
about how awful cold April can be,
how hard it is to believe
that five minutes ago
we put a good man in the ground
and then came back here
to take our place in line.

Steven Schild

Something for a Son

A man awash in womanness
awaiting the outcome
of an act of love,
lone man attending the birth.
My heart is in the right place
but my equipment is all wrong,
all thumbs, all arms and elbows
in this hothouse of skyward-knifing knees
and heart-shaped hips, a garden
of women in which I can do nothing
for my son but say this:
"Be stronger of heart
than of arm.
Be first to extend a hand
after anger.
Neither run from thunder
nor take lightning lightly.
Look life in the eye.
Behold and believe
all that is good.
Be ready for the rest.
Be worth all this.
Be worth all this."

Steven Schild

The Bride

Ceremony over
she was buckboarded
to a flatland farmhouse
with a cast-iron cookstove
and a garden that wasn't.
She raised chickens and children,
swept and scoured as if possessed,
made meals from damn little
and one day brought breakfast
only to him,
and then to an empty table
where her own cooking
had the taste of
meat boiled too long.

"You have to get out,"
so she did,
senior-citizen dances in town
and a spot of hope-chest rouge,
paper corsage from the craft class
and a row of folding chairs,
again a shy girl
in a wallflower line
knock-kneed with dread
at never being asked
or being asked
far too soon.

Steven Schild

Heirlooms

This tattered chair is where Grandpa when young
collapsed like bursting seed upon learning
of the child to come, maybe a son,

one more gift from she who shared his yearning
as she searched for lines in this mottled mirror
as signs she was helplessly turning

into the woman every girl fears.
So he bought this faded bow for her hair
to show that he didn't care for the years

gone, that his heart would ever find her fair
as on that first morning of long-ago spring
when that shiest boy couldn't help but stare

as she, in rough gingham, walked out to bring
water to those burning men—and in doing so
taught us to know the holiness of humble things.

Steven Schild

At the Kitchen Table on the Anniversary of a Death

A year later
it still hurt
like a deep cut,
a wound fresh as
the bottomless bounty of her garden
in the sharp sunshine of early
September, spilling as would
an autumn-ripe tomato
cut with a canning knife
clean in two.

Tears for the moment gone,
we find balm in talk
of the glory of her garden,
brilliant symmetry of gladiola,
fatness of squash and final potatoes,
plump, thumping music of ripe melon,
we find succor in the savor
of this good, good earth,
and all we have taken therefrom,
and all that we owe it, each one.

Steven Schild

Plato wrote that even the best poets are, at best, imitators thrice removed. If that's true, then imagine how far off they might be in trying to explain how they do their work. I get nervous writing about poetic process because the chances for error or delusion are so great. Even the most precise account written by the most talented poet can't explain what happens in writing a poem. Yes, there are inspirations, images in laser-like moments that make the beginning or end or central idea of a poem. But the other details are as varied as the shapes of clouds or clumps of dirt. We don't know what goes into making a poem that works.

Houseman observed that he sometimes wrote poems after returning from a walk in the woods with a pint, but that he couldn't tell if the poems' quality was due to the woods or the pint.

And so it is with most poetry—we can't name or know for sure what makes a good poem. My chances are best when I write about something I know and care about. But I'm often not the best judge of what's my best work. I prefer to leave the analysis and explanation to someone more articulate than I. What matters most is the poem itself. And the truly good poem speaks for itself, not by telling, not by showing, but by being what it is.

(Self-Portrait)

For the past three years **Kathleen Heideman** has been working on a long poem set in a landscape of abandoned iron mines. "I was a poet," she says, "utterly without epic ambitions—a simple probing of heartache, that's all I wanted to write. The poem, however, took another route, leading me down beyond the strictly personal scars, into rich sublayers of geology, earth scars, Jungian descents, defunct mines, oracular mythology, metallurgy and alchemy, environmental loss, and the historical particulars of a few small towns in the Lake Superior Iron Range."

Raised on a farm in Wisconsin, she moved to Minneapolis in the late 1980's. She has won several awards, including a 1999 Bush Fellowship in Literature, a Minnesota State Arts Board Fellowship, a Loft-McKnight Fellowship in Poetry, and the Richard Eberhart Poetry Prize. Her manuscript *Migration of Icarus* was named a finalist for the 1998 Marianne Moore Poetry Prize and the 1998 Aldrich Museum Emerging Poets Award. Between stanzas, she is a Computer Learning specialist and Computer Imaging teacher at the Minneapolis College of Art and Design.

A Field of Mudswallows

Once upon a time, a miner undermined Cornishtown
until his own home slowly sank into the basement floor:
Down!—down, into the caving-in ground.

On Snow Street, gardens grew unstable and playgrounds
gave way beneath their teeter-totters. Today, the rusting signs warn
DANGER—KEEP OUT. By danger, we mean "Caving Ground"

—just an empty, ordinary-looking meadow now,
a field of mudswallows and sumac and cement porches
where *(Once upon a time)* a miner undermined his own hometown

like a nutworm, moving from the heart-out, tearing down
wide hematite columns for their ore, those underground supports
that were a sort of spine, deep down, bracing up the Caving Grounds.

Once upon a time, a miner removed his own spine, which sounds
absurd unless you've seen the earth swallow yards, flagpoles, front doors.
This is no fairy tale: *The Miner Who Undermined His Own Hometown—*

It was his job. So his lawn dropped several feet; his house was zoned "unsound"
and the foundation razed. Perhaps there's no redeeming moral to the story
of how, once upon a recent time, a miner undermined this town.
Perhaps we drop without a solid reason: down, down into the Caving Grounds.

Kathleen Heideman

Lost Gospel of Infancy

Fear not, and I will call the weak worm from its lowly bed,
and thou shalt hear its voice.
William Blake

She started out like any baby, adored
by strangers, showered with their gifts,
sucking happily in the lap of a pure woman;
a milk that formed large ideas in her head
—those who bore witness to the first months
claim they did not see the change, no voice
dropping loud from the clouds, no bushes
burning,

but sheepfarmers began their gossip: an aura
they claimed, which illuminates her pale head.
By evening, the infant stood in her crib
and walked on miniature feet—walked perfectly!
And in the morning was found beside the road
with her legs folded into the shape of a flower,
scratching at the dust with a twig,
writing:

like a lamb giving birth to a ewe, they laughed,
words so large they'll catch in her little throat!
One day, to illustrate a complicated point,
she crossed herself and cut an earthworm into halves.
You see, she said to the gathering crowd,
this cut worm is forgiving the plow.
She held up the wormhalves for inspection, and
all fell silent, straining to hear. The worm said
nothing,

but stained each upraised palm with its stigmata.
Thus were unrecorded miracles performed, dismissed
as a girl's first attempts at magic. And she grew lonely
even as she grew in wisdom. Imagine those hours stirring water,
kneading dust into a living paste, forming mudbirds
with her fingers, using her tiny nails to carve each beak, eye,
feather; clapping to see the work of her own hands,
flying—

Kathleen Heideman

Villanelle for a Negaunee Oracle

"Though there have been literally hundreds of millions of tons of iron mined in Negaunee, the first ton has yet to be mined on the strength of a diploma, a poem, Shakespearean English or the manners of a Vanderbilt."
Ernie Ronn

It all begins with loss: a sudden lack-of-bearing;
compass fingers spin until they find the greed within us.
It all begins with rust: an egg of hematite plucked from an outcropping,

and from the mine we dug to mark that holy spot, an oracle was singing
"Down! down,"—so down we went, where Dante flew for Beatrice,
where it might begin with iron after all, with Hematite, with him descending

like a blackened penitent into the grotto where he heard Iron singing
like a rusty bird in a cave of windy bells. Where he worshiped, yes,
but left her weeping later. Such men gain from loss, a sudden bearing

down of flesh, a lightless kiss when rock explodes and blasting
sticks discharge so Iron crumbles into softness at his fierce embrace.
It all requires an iron fist, below, Pure Hematite, a mirror reflecting

the work of men who built Negaunee from stones they were stealing
from the sacristy of Iron. Didn't they see Her, watching in the darkness?
All their theft must end in rust, when they've finished ransacking

the cathedral. "Foundation, house, faith"—ferrous images he's painting
on a pale egg. Later, hungry: he'll crack the shell and leave another mess.
It all ends in profit-&-loss: Ore abandoned for the high cost of its extracting.
Further down the hole, a rusty bird guards her ruined nest, still singing.

As I said, it all begins with loss.

Kathleen Heideman

How the Abandoned Lands Speak

Moses, descending the mountain, returned with stone tablets—
    the Old Law.
This is the New Law: *finding an old cabin, high upon the mountain,*
    disturb nothing.

Reaching the first blank page of your sketchbook, record a rough
    outline of the deflated
boards, the yawn of the shaft mouth barred only by beamlitter where
    the headframe,

leaning, a working man's Tower of Pisa, finally toppled on the hole.
    Survey in silence
what remains—silence, the way we learned to pray. Selecting a section
    of earth,

ask yourself some sort of question that cannot be answered within the
    spin of an hour:
what can we learn, for example, *by inspecting the details of failure?*

Adherence does not guarantee success. The shaft is not too deep
—down just far enough so air, sinking, uncirculating for years, has
    gone bad:

soured by monoxide, pocketing itself along the drift as so many bitter
    worms cocoon
their metamorphing forms to stone. It's a shallow hole, a short drift.
    And fatal.

Haven't you ever believed—*for a few weeks, at least?*—that a life of
    honest working
would pay off? Privately, each tongue knows the good, salty flavor of
    our own sweat,

or the metal taste of blood, that throbbing knuckle we dumbly
    hammered open
then sucked to staunch the flow? Although it's true we later lost the
    vein, digging,

Kathleen Heideman

or maybe the ore never assayed as richly as we hoped—to sell the
    failed venture,
we might have to salt the mine, using a shotgun to fire real gold dust,
    impregnating

the poor walls with shimmer, a promise clearly visible to anyone who
    might buy . . .
Admit it. Under the Old Law, how many lies did we profit by?

Come Sunday

we'll be down in the basement at Saint Tom's
watching the children put on their Passion play—an end,
finally, to their month of wonderings: *how long does it take to bleed
to death? how tall is a life-sized cross? which spices were used to marinate
the dead? how heavy was the stone & who rolled from the tomb?*
Ah, well. We'll just follow the plot as best we can, knowing
how Jesus and Judas will be played this year by the Olson brothers,
those identical twins whose own mother admits she can barely tell
    the boys
apart, at that distance—*though if you listen closely to the dialogue*
she promised us yesterday, waiting in the check-out line,
it'll all make perfect sense.

Kathleen Heideman

Signs and Signifiers

I'd hold my breath whenever we neared Royalton
Cemetery's wrought-iron gate and the graveyard billboard's
eternal (peeling) message: *CHRIST IS THE ANSWER
—WHAT IS YOUR QUESTION?*

Then whisper blasphemous questions in my sister's
younger ear: *Okay, Esther—how many stars?
how many bullheads in the Embarrass?
how many stones, I'm talking total stones,
in all the fencerows of Lebanon township?*

Or the mystery most central to my young soul:
why did dinosaurs go extinct? Gracie-to-my-George,
she'd pause to think before each answer: *Christ?*
then *Christ!* my father would interrupt us, righteous,
somebody ought to fertilize these damn fields!

True, the corn around Royalton grew shorter than our wont.
Poor soil, I'd answer him, somber. I knew about things like that.
Even in the billboard's cooler shadow, cornleaves curled
toward heaven. *Except those outer rows of corn, I mean.
Nearer to the graves, and greener than the rest.*

Kathleen Heideman

About eight years ago, the world's largest living organism was discovered growing in the Iron Mountain area: it is a single subterranean fungus, a living maze inhabiting several square acres, revealing itself through mushrooms (and spores) sent up like fingers to the surface. Like that organism, my long poem The Caving Grounds *is a single body, but not a single poem—rather, after the Greek* eidyllion, *it contains small idylls, villanelles, and self-contained segments that, together, create the whole.* The Caving Grounds narratives are fragmented, an orebody blasted from its bedrock context, a non-linear amalgamate whose excavated strata include heartache, geological rakings, the rusting artifacts of consumerism, the solace of landscape, the inherent value and danger in 'descent,' the evolution of mining technology, the environmental cost of 150 years of iron mining, the sympathetic relationship between minescape and moonscape, landmarks, and the spiritual affinities between abandoned mines, oracular caves, spiritual grottoes, monkholes, cathedral vaults, etc.

I follow the tracks of the common packrat: old letters, photographs, a box of rusted metal scraps, ore samples, shards of window glass, broken tools, etc. I begin with the personal, the fetishized, the kitsch, the surreal, the mystical. Normally, I live with this debris until it is as close as my own thoughts—then reshape it into poetry. I work my will upon the material. This time, however, the poem is working its will upon me. The poem demands that I move outward, downwards, away from "me" and into empathy. As though traversing a field seeing only benign surface, I begin writing unaware of its deep intentions, its sudden openings and shudders and uncapped shafts, its vast subterranean chambers. I am the visitor, stumbling into the presence of the subject, humbled by all that I do not know. I know that I am "discovering" what has been known to others, but never recorded.

My approach is interdisciplinary: text, sound, images stirred into meaning.

(Photo by Tom Foley)

Michael Dennis Browne left his native England for Iowa City in 1965 and has lived in Minneapolis since 1971. As poet, professor, and mentor of poets (including some published here) he is highly honored by those who know his work. His two most recent books are *Selected Poems 1965–1995* and *You Won't Remember This* (both Carnegie Mellon University Press publications). He has won several awards and has written many texts for music. Forthcoming publications include a chapbook in the "Greatest Hits" series from Pudding House, and "Give Her the River," a picture book with paintings by Wendell Minor (Atheneum, 2003).

Hide and Go Seek

(For Lisa)

I count to fifty.
Then I appear at the French window;
in my hand, the three-flame candelabrum.
The children have run to hide in my sister's garden.
It is March, damp dark, that English dark I left.

I make the monster sound.
I give the groan they long to hear, and fear.
I can almost feel their shivering out there.

Then I begin to move.
I lurch, stiff-legged. I sway.
I am the Mud Man, come
still smeared from his swamp,
I am something extinct
with my rotting fingers,
I am the slimy thing from the sea
who leaks after them on feet
horribly like the human hand, but heavier.
I am he no longer afraid of fire,
who points these prongs of flame to find them.
I need some blood.
I need to catch me some family flesh
and chew it down to the bone.

Appalled, they hurtle all over,
the nephews, nieces,
they scatter, they stream
round Fran and Angela's garden,
desperate scared, mad scared—
who let this thing loose in England?—
run! run!—
the Bogey Man, the Bog Beast—
run! run!

Michael Dennis Browne

Roaring, reaching out,
again and again I miss them,
so slow I am,
so sleepy with my swampy blood,
miss them just enough to freshen their fear,
to send them screaming further
into the dark,
out behind the beanpoles,
behind the compost,
behind the favorite tree that is now
metal to the touch.
I hear, I hear the panting.

And—it is enough. Now it is done.
Now I raise the candles to show
my friendlier face—I am Michael again,
the almost American uncle,
and I call to them: "All in, All in."
Together we go toward the house,
through the garden that is theirs again,
laughing, still thrilled with our fright.
And Damien, my godson, four,
that boy of light I sought in the dark,
shouts: "I'm bigger than myself!"

Whoever the seekers, children,
whoever will chase you,
if inside you, if behind you,
may they miss, I pray it,
may they not touch,
may you make it
past such grasping and reach the house
as now together we do,
where people are waiting who love us
and from the darkness welcome us.
O mystery of family. O darkness. O house.
I pray it: *All in. All in.*

Michael Dennis Browne

Tree Care

I go up to them, the tree care crew—
    first the young man in green,
and ask, over the noise of the generator,
    what's the name of that tree,
the one flowering everywhere right now—
    there's one down there at the corner—
with those cones of whitish-yellow blossom
    that smell unbelievably sweet;
can't tell you, he says, go ask the girls,
    they know more about these things.

I approach the young woman in green.
    I've got our mild-looking dog with me,
but also I've got my beard, my silvery beard,
    and I ask, and she looks a little annoyed,
as if she thinks I'm weird,
    as if I'm trying to come on to her,
and she frowns and shakes her head.
    There's another young worker beyond her,
but I let it go, walk on.

The tree care crew is pumping
    something into the elms to save them;
I'll bet they're familiar with the name "elm"
    and, for sure, the name of the poison,
but not with what I want to know.
    (I don't need to know, but I want to
and will. If this fragrance were a face,
    I swear I'd stand like an idiot
and stare and stare.)

When I get home, maybe my wife,
    who's used to my ways,
will be awake enough by now to tell me
    what smells so sweet.

Michael Dennis Browne

Evensong

"There he is" he learns to say
when we glimpse the great sun burning down
toward the hill, and "There she is"
when we spot the pale enormous moon
floating low above the pines;
and over and over, swiveling his head,
he says it as I drive them both,
daughter and son, around the roads
until they sleep, so I can have
dinner and an hour alone with their mother.

Ahead in the shadows, two deer.
A little further, metal abandoned
in somebody's yard, auto parts
and ancient appliances, that later
the moon will make into something,
that same skilled stranger keeping us
company beyond the branches.

He wants to know why they share the sky,
and all I can tell him is it's a secret
we have to guess at as we go;
and "There he is" he says once more
as the hill prepares to swallow fire,
and "There she is" as she climbs the air,
and murmurs and murmurs until he sleeps
(and she already is sleeping.)

Michael Dennis Browne

The Now, the Long Ago

In the dream time of the swarming snow
We're on the couch, just chatting, you and I,
Here in the now, there in the long ago.

The world outside is singular and slow,
As if the winter taught all things to sigh
In the dream time of the swarming snow.

I'll make our supper, then we'll watch a show,
And then you'll choose some stories, by and by,
Here in the now, there in the long ago.

So many things that you don't need to know
About the years, the years that multiply
In the dream time of the swarming snow.

This won't go on forever, child, although
I've never had the words to tell you why,
Here in the now, there in the long ago,

Won't be for always, little love, and so
We'll take this all as blessing, you and I,
In the dream time of the swarming snow,
Here in the now, there in the long ago.

Michael Dennis Browne

Mengele

Don't tell me about the bones of Mengele,
the bones are alive and well.
Don't think to thrill me with tales
of the drowned bones uncovered,
the bones are alive and well
inside the sleeves of a suit this day
and carving out the figures of a fat check
or severing a ribbon with the ceremonial scissors
or holding the head of a child;
I tell you, the bones are alive and well.

Don't expect me to get excited
concerning the skull of Mengele,
the skull is alive and well,
the skull is asquirm with schemes this day
and low words are leaving it at this moment
and other skulls are nodding at what they hear,
seated about the world table;
I tell you, the skull is alive and well.

Don't bother showing me pictures
of the remains of Mengele,
the remains are alive and well
and simmering in our rivers
or climbing into our houses out of the ground
where they will not be confined
or sliding inside the rain
out of the summer air, oh yes,
the remains are even there, I tell you,
are alive, are well, are everywhere.

Michael Dennis Browne

As for poetry, I continue to pursue it as passionately, I believe, *as ever, finding it always elusive, while also pursuing other loves, libretto and article and children's novel loves, but acknowledging poetry, if I am obliged to, as my first love, my chief one. In the sixth collection I am presently working on,* Things I Can't Tell You, *I am trying, now in my sixtieth year, to go deeper into some ongoing obsessions, among them England and family and children and love and social justice and the land of the north woods and, at the same time, give voice to some things I have had somewhat little success in articulating, among them married love, spiritual beliefs, and my own brands of hidden and semi-hidden madnesses.*

When Jim Moore asked me if there was anything in particular I wanted him to say when he introduced me at the reading of my just-published Selected Poems *a year or two ago, the one thing I came up with was that I had kept faith with poetry. And so I have, in my own fickle way, for now almost forty years—the fortieth anniversary of my father's death, the event which, above all, precipitated me into poetry, being three months away. Poetry tantalizes me—Chaucer's "the life so short, the craft so long to learn" indeed—but I love it in a very complete way and rely on it, both as reader and writer, as a conduit for complexities of thought and feeling not available in any other form, including the utterly magnificent art of music.*

My plan is to stay playful, stay alert and flickering inside, even as certain inevitable processes begin to make my body offers it finds it cannot refuse. The psyche, Jung said in an interview once, does not intend to die. For my part, I have no sense that the imagination will ever die, but an expectation that words will, at some point, drop away from the process. Until that time, here I am, as much in love with the whole mystery of it as I ever have been, just humbled, finally and thank God, by a sense of the immensity of it, and the privilege of being a player.

(Photo by Asame Murakami)

Orval Lund grew up in Lancaster, a town in the far northwestern corner of Minnesota. There he worked on farms and in his parents' store, trucked grain and bread, and later he did time in a canning factory and the army. His education at several universities eventually led to a long career as professor at Winona State University. Many students and the writing community of southeastern Minnesota have benefited from his commitment to the writing life.

Lund served as editor of *Great River Review* for many years. His first collection of poetry, *Casting Lines*, was recently published by New Rivers Press.

Plowing

Crawling steady at a slight slant,
smooth waves of sliced and shiny earth spiraling
behind, the engine droning, the floor-hum tickling
your feet, the big yellow Moline fenders
defining your cabin, you're much alone
on flat fields, not a tree in sight, seagulls,
a punctuation in the sky, hovering
for worms sliced and tossed atop.

At field's end, you jerk the frayed rope to raise
the plow. The shiny, scoured blades climb
out, the tractor takes its little step
up to sod, sighing from its upright pipe, and you turn
and steer your right wheel toward
the clean square trough, then jerk the cord to drop
the plow; the tractor grunts, hunkers
down, squares its shoulders, snorts and starts again.

Again, the engine's drone, the scrape
of stone on steel. You can feel
your back relax, the tingle in your feet, can smell
dark earth and remember a day
you prepared the field for growth,
the rolling sod streaming back and scouring
shares to a shine, the poetry
of straight black lines across a flat field.

Orval Lund

For John, Who Did Not Choose Baseball

Because I loved the bone-white hardness of the ball
that fit like a perfect toy in my hand,
the way my fingers ratcheted its tight red seams,
as if I could wind up joy and let it fly,
the running under the spinning ball
popped up in a child-blue sky,
its satisfying thunk into my glove,
the around-the-horn with other boys,
I wanted so badly to give it you

a seven year-old lefty behind the house,
whose loose control burned my face red
and led me to zip the ball back into your tears.
But we kept on, a tyrant reigning behind a cardboard plate,
a subject red-handed. And you,
at your first and last game, standing
on the raised mound, the game spinning
around you like a merry-go-round gone mad,
the ball large and sour as a grapefruit in your hand,
missing the plate pitch after pitch,
I gripping the wire fence with white hands,
the white-haired coach shouting angry words
until he took you out, the bases loaded.

Now, at fourteen, out you go,
like a thoroughbred garbed in blue silks,
your baggy old-time hat tilted jauntily,
your lean legs loping across open fields.
I try to keep up but can't, and marvel
at the nervous grace of your long body.
When I see you, the cemetery milestone turned,
running back to me, you smile and wave
your open hands, and I, yes, I
garbed in my drab clothes of guilt and age, yes,
I smile and open my hands to you.

Take Paradise

Pave paradise, put up a parking lot.
—Joni Mitchell

A willowy swamp once stewed just off
the highway by the lake, till KMart
came to town like an invading army
and drained it, dumped in sand and clay,
smoothed it out, laid Tarmac, and opened
for business. Now people can't wait to file
in to vote under flashing blue lights
to "Blowin' in the Wind" by 101 Strings. Seeds

of the purple loosestrife have blown
away, cattails puffed up and off.
Red-winged blackbirds lingered,
dove awhile, shit on cars, then left
the broth of the swamp seeping underground
to some oven waiting there, and you drive past
and glare, oh how you glare and feel some satisfaction
that you don't shop there. Floating

in the gloaming, this thirty-thousand-square-
foot cement block rectangle squats its atomic pile
behind its huge sign—kayo, strikeout, king
of the hill—and the sun shines even
hotter, the earth dizzy as ever, and you
walk the edge of the parking lot and sniff for swamp
but get only stale popcorn and textile chemicals
tinted with exhaust as a new stew brews, before

you enter the blue light, the night of half-alive
ghouls, mirrored sunglasses, bulging polyester pockets, gray,
cratered faces of the moon, and clean
Taiwan shoes, for it's warm here, a community altar
of our common denominator. What an effort
it takes to lift off
this anchor of the human spirit, where you can get
the cheapest batteries in town.

Orval Lund

Swede Decides to Quit Hunting

God holding still and letting it happen again,
and again and again.
—William Stafford

Once, out walking the woods with a shotgun
looking for grouse to shoot, wading
through brambles that tugged at his arms and legs
like so many electrical cords strung with sharp sparks
that stung through his long-sleeved shirt,
his double-lined trousers, scratched thin red lines
like his kitten at home,
              Swede almost stepped
on something that flew up onto the stem of a bramble
at chest height, a tiny owl, silent,
golden in the morning haze, blinking
at him, unseeing, eyes deep as night's back,
as a time when Swede's forebears clustered in cold caves,
huddled against darkness.
              Swede blinked back.
Time stopped, took a deep breath, maybe looked about.
Then Swede lifted his gun barrel,
held its open steel mouth that could screech hot flames,
acrid smoke, almost against the bird's chest.
It still blinked back, blind and fearless,
softly feathered fist.

The moment trembled,
a drunk about to stagger,
or a babe about to take its first step,
till Swede touched the steel circle to the owl's chest
and up the owl opened
into a hand that flew,
quiet as God.

Men in Winter

stand out on the ice
over their holes, augers
laid beside them, dipping
sieves to keep the blackness
liquid, jigging hooks
that pierce icy minnows
fathoms below
in the utter dark, their lines
growing like wicks being tallowed,
freezing foot and thumb
for some walleye dumb enough to suck
their hook, and to pull
it forth from the mystery
below. They come
in twos or threes or all alone,
and stand mute. Try to strike
up some talk and they barely look
up, continue to diddle with their rods.
Sometimes you meet them
in their dark hoods as they leave
the ice, and you greet them
but they won't react, sluggish
as bullheads forty feet deep,
secretive as Mississippi bottom
muck, unwilling to share
the secret of their hot hole
where they caught one skinny perch.

But try this: walk down the street
of any town and smile at women.
Make it a nice, sweet smile. Most
will smile back like Samoa,
liquid as surf, sweet as mahimahi.
Listen to a gathering of women
with no men around. I have
done so, as a child,
to Mama's whist club. Down
stairs would hush as jokes

Orval Lund

were told, then gales
of laughter nearly rose
my grate, my floor. Or
my wife's book club,
as I, banished to the bedroom,
try to read, rings such talk and laughter
the very springs tingle in sympathy.
Away from men (what relief it must be),
they will blossom like eulalia japonica
after a monsoon, from rich humus,
under warm sun, and caress one another
with words, words, words, till they come
with gales of laughter that rise
and fall like tides. God I love 'em,
the women. Who drive me out
onto the ice.

So what makes a good poem?

A good poem must be engaged with its subject—and felt. Even the most overworked subject (Grandma's funeral) can make a good poem if the poet is vitally connected to and feels the subject. Conventional reactions do not make a poem.

A good poem respects and cares deeply about the language. A poet is one who considers language a tool that can be manipulated, played around with, experimented with. A good poem seeks the best word, used as if it doesn't carry hundreds of years of dust on its back.

A good poem is awake. This above else I look for in a poem. Life can be bitter and it's easy to sink into a slough of despond (not easy to be there, but to sink). It's easy to chase pleasure and evade the whole issue of being an alert, thoughtful, caring human being. But a poem is awake to what it is to be human and engaged with the world.

A good poem discovers something. Robert Frost said, "No surprise for the writer, no surprise for the reader."

Finally, though it is seldom talked about, any long-term engagement, any long-term commitment to poetry is an exercise in character. So live well, though I can't tell you how to do that.

Bill Meissner, Director of Creative Writing at St. Cloud State University, has won several awards for his poetry, including a NEA Creative Writing Fellowship, a Loft-McKnight Award and a Minnesota State Arts Board Fellowship. His three books of poetry are *Learning to Breathe Underwater* and *The Sleepwalker's Son* (both published by University of Ohio Press), and *Twin Sons of Different Mirrors* (with Jack Driscoll, Milkweed Editions). Random House also published (and Southern Methodist University Press reprinted) a widely-read collection of baseball fiction entitled *Hitting into the Wind.*

First Ties: The Father in the Mirror

Fourteen, late for church, I stood in front of the mirror, fumbling
with the new tie until my father's face surfaced behind me.
Reaching in front of my chest, he led
the red and blue silk around and
under, under and
around in some mysterious
pattern. *Nothing to a tie*, he said.

For those few seconds, his big arms were my arms—
I watched the thick fingers
working the tie, each time a little
too short or too long.

He leaned his face alongside mine,
and I smelled a sharp scent of Old Spice, heard the hiss of sighs
through his nose, like a car tire losing air,
as he focused on the broad wrinkled pillar
that would not tie.
Arms that hadn't surrounded me for years
now wrapped me like ribbons. His elbows swung
like rhythmic pendulums, and
for an instant it looked like we could have been
dancing, so I stood still,
unable to pull away from the rough kiss of whiskers
against my smooth cheek.

He finally finished a crooked knot, slid it
up to my tender throat, too tight, too tight.
Just right, he said.
Then I understood
that being an adult meant
you looked a little older, but you couldn't breathe.
>   I watched my father
>   back away in the mirror and
>   disappear, and all I could see was myself,
>   the knot at my throat, a soft, angled
>   embrace of cloth.

Bill Meissner

The Father, Who Could Not Swim

Morning was a mouthful of water
when I first learned of dying:
Kaufman's dad was fishing when he tipped
his aluminum boat. He never heard
the shouts that flattened
on the ripples above him; he was sinking
deep into the blue waltz
of the lake
(the way my father did
when he folded the newspaper filled with wars
in half, in half
again, then pressed his creased forehead
miles into his pillow).

Somewhere a knife shreds the night
like barracuda, a bullet punctures a quiet brain
like a sliver from a nightmare:
(whatever kills another man's flesh
numbs the skin on my father's wrist).

Still brushing my teeth before school,
I heard dad's deep breaths
behind me. I knew he wanted
to rest his leaden palm on my shoulder,
but in the bathroom mirror I watched
his wavy reflection slowly turning,
the screen door closing behind him like an eyelid.

Bill Meissner

The Contortionist

For him, any position is fine:
his heel resting casually on his shoulder,
bread dough arms twisting together.
He could even compress himself
into a two by two foot cardboard box,
still have room
to eat shredded wheat from a bowl, people
pointing and laughing above him
as he chews.

He has almost begun to enjoy arching his body
into an exact O, to feel
the breeze, the universe as it blows
through the open porthole of himself.
He knows this is his fate: to be loved,
to be remembered most
for becoming something he is not—
a chair, the entire alphabet, the ripples
on top of water.
Over the years, he has learned to erase
the wince, learned to relax
with his legs wrapped around his neck,
a thick noose.

For a final stunt, bending
backwards, a spatula between his teeth,
he flips pancakes,
listens to the floppy applause.

Alone in the dressing room
he sits naked on the floor.
Somehow he is nearly comfortable
as he wraps his whole body carefully
into a large, pink bow.
Yes, he thinks, this is his gift to himself.

Bill Meissner

The Contortionist's Wife

She knows him, yet she doesn't always recognize him—
some mornings she finds him in the kitchen cupboard
flattened among the cereal boxes,
some evenings he's folded beneath her chair
when she sits down for dinner.
Once he surprised her when he rose from the washing machine tub
like a genie, gave her three wishes
and a box of Cheer.

Some days she doesn't know if he's shaping himself
or if she's shaping him. All she knows is the way
he twists her emotions: he makes her laugh, he makes her cry.

She's not sure if it's funny that he
could be lying between the sheets of her bed without her
noticing him.
Sometimes he's closer to her than she ever imagined, like the
tub full of warm bath water she slides herself into.
Sometimes he's distant, pinpricks of stars in the night sky.
But most often he's both near and far, lifting himself
from the vase in the corner, his smile full of flowers.

Ah, she wishes she could be a contortionist, too.
She wishes she could be the one to surprise him
some morning, disguising herself as the wheat bread
popping from the toaster
or the coat rack as he reaches for his jacket.
She gazes at her stiff flesh with the brittle bones inside,
thinking if only she could slip herself around his finger
like a ring he didn't know he was wearing
for the rest of his life.

Bill Meissner

The Education of Martin Halsted

We taught you, Martin. In sixth grade the three of us taught
your marshmallow hands to harden,
taught your cheeks the color of bruises.
In the alley behind a wooden shed,
one by one we punched your face
until the eggs of your eyes broke.

You never wanted to fight anyone.
It's just that your face was a window
we always wanted to fling a rock through.
In junior high you moved to another town.
Your mother sent you to an institution—
weird in the head, everyone said.

Last time I saw you was sophomore year at the theatre.
Back for the weekend, you told me
how much you loved to draw circles with a pen
on the back of your left hand.
You held it toward me:
too close in the near dark, you smudged my cheek.

Sometimes, when I go back to town,
I drive up and down that alley.
Sometimes I want to get out
of the car, rub my palm on the shed,
feel the slivers searching.

The three of us are grown now, work in different cities.
Though we don't know it, Martin, you're the reason
we can't fall asleep some nights.
And in the mornings, our hands on the wheel,
you're the scars on our knuckles
we never grew out of.

Bill Meissner

The Secrets of America

They die and are born and go on dying,
their feet never leaving their yards.
Mornings, they spread their margarine smoothly,
don't remember the darkness that pooled
in the backs of their skulls while they slept.
They put extra cream in their coffee.

Fathers and mothers won't mention their sons drive
on country roads at night without headlights,
daughters lift pleated skirts
above their heads like overcast skies.
Everyone believes the ghosts of their ancestors enter
through their shoes as they garden.
They picture themselves walking barefoot near the church.
Downtown, young wives gaze through their reflections
at naked mannequins.

Before dinner, they brown their roasts
on both sides. Recipes are funneled into electrical wires,
squeezed along by the feet of blackbirds.
In time, they'll tell you, their houses will
sink into the ground until the whole town's
a flat plain again,
a place for pioneers to discover.
They'll tell you this is America
idling in their garages, America steaming on their plates.

America in their back yards,
like trousers hanging on the clothesline in the wind,
the hollow legs climbing
and dancing and
falling still all afternoon.

I can best describe my process of writing/inspiration by using analogies to sound and light. Sometimes, significant images or memories are like tuning forks perpetually humming inside me. All I have to do is listen. Other times, an idea emerges as a small crack of light that's shining through from my unconscious mind. It might merely be a single sentence or an image that's asking to be developed into a poem. The writer's job is to expand that narrow space of light into a window, to crawl in, and then to climb back out with an armful of words and, ultimately, share that poem with the reader.

I believe that writers should write about what's important in their lives. I find myself writing most about experiences and relationships, and my poems are always a delicate blend of truth and fiction based on those experiences.

(Photo by Liadan McKiernan)

Ethna McKiernan moved to St. Paul from Dublin, Ireland, when she was eight years old. "Forty years later, I'm still in Minnesota." She wrote her first poems as a teenager, hitchhiked through Europe in the early 1970's "despite what my parents said about opium dens in Amsterdam," came back to drive a school bus in St. Paul, and worked her way into a business importing and distributing Irish books in the U.S. Her first book of poetry, *Caravan,* was a Minnesota Book Award nominee in 1990, and her second, *The One Who Swears You Can't Start Over,* is due out in 2001 from Salmon Poetry in Ireland. Currently she lives in Minneapolis with her two teenage sons.

Homage to the Common

How I love the blazing dailyness
of this world, the way my shoes
wear down their heels in the same spot
each year; the gene-print of freckles
on my children's cheeks, the plain truth
that dust-balls breed, regardless;
the unmade beds and other signs
of absent domesticity, the late-night hum
of the furnace pumping out its heat,
even the knots in my shoulders
I've known since childhood.

I celebrate alike the lumpy August lawn
awash with acorns and the first new snow
which tempers any memory of wrong;
my aging Ford Escort and the slush
that city buses sling across its windshield,
the pageantry of light each morning
from the east, strong coffee
halved by cream; that in these last late years
of the 20th century, this planet
keeps on spinning toward some destiny
beyond our knowing. And always

How utterly my friends astonish me
with their simple ordinary faith and care
for this or that. For the common grace
of all of it, the way the earth's
relentless lovely roots pull us deeper
in, I offer blessings, praise,
amazement.

Ethna McKiernan

The Other Woman

You visit her house for the first time without him.
She offers you tea, a still-warm jar of raspberry jam,
kindness to trouble your insides.
Later you walk outdoors into the perfect garden
and it is too clear that the apple trees
have been tended carefully for years,
for they are verging on their first green fruit.
Everything here, in fact, has roots.

Inside now her children fan about her
like blue stones in a peacock's upraised tail,
and every facet of each gem
throws back his reflection, too.
It is too beautiful, too cruel.

At night he comes to you once more
and you are not innocent,
knowing precisely where
to place your hands upon his back
while he breaks his loneliness inside you.

So you hold him, you hold his past, you hold
the faint shadow of his wife
which staggers there between you,
you hold a gift of jam
and an empty, outstretched hand,
awake, thinking of her,
even as she thinks of you.

Ethna McKiernan

Those We Carry with Us

Not the vendor selling hot roasted chestnuts,
sweet as the mashed white meat inside
the broken shell is. Not the man himself,
his Rastafarian braids electric as his smile.
Not the kindly mayor of our childhoods,
gaily tossing candy from the one-car float
of small-town Halloween.

                Even the dead we lose,
eventually, pieces of them slipping from our arms
against our wills, like heavy trays we can
no longer hold. A glass breaks; we go on,
sewing the sharp pebble of loss safely into hems
or pockets. All our lives elaborate distractions
will fret for our attention, papers beckon,
sirens call our names. For all our ignorance
we know what's worth holding onto, can sense
whom we're bound to, if not why—

                My Polish friend
of the exquisite poems, the blue tattooed number
throbbing on her wrist as she held my hand
in both of hers somewhere in Los Angeles
while I cried; the travelling man I gave my soul
to at nineteen; the small angel of innocence
who guards me when the darkness comes;
the boys' shouts outside the kitchen window
and their faces later, deep in velvet sleep;
strangers, whose intimate connection
was made holy by a single glance;

                These are the ones
who walk with us, bound lightly as the sheen
of cobweb lacing the hibiscus tree, bound tightly
over matter, distance, birth. In my dreams
I see them trailing in the shadows of the horses,
silent in the desert night. I finger the strands
which link them to my caravan and marvel
at such wealth. They are my crew, my absolutes.
I will carry them with me, always.

Ethna McKiernan

The Architecture of Flowers

Inside the drum of petals
yellow-cropped stamens
shake gold dust from anthers.
They are a stand of miniature trees,
tall as thumbnails, wide
as a strand of hair.
If I could pull myself up
their silky ropes, I would leap
into the rouged bowl
of this orange columbine
and wander through the chambers
of its complicated heart
until I reached the room
of childhood, where I would taste
again my father's oatmeal
in the chilly Dublin kitchen
before dawn, breathe
my mother's lily-of-the-valley smell
at bathtime, unknow roses
sheared off by the storm
or the bitter rages
of the father of my children.
And in that room
I would freeze, raise
my arms high as irises,
hard as trumpet blasts, urge
the whole future
to stop, now, at once.

Ethna McKiernan

At This Moment

And if I have nothing to say
and all the words inside my brain
are hollowed out, scraped clean, gone,
then let nothingness stream forth
in rows of blazing zeroes.
Let emptiness be the still lake it is
where I coast in my small boat
fishing for the thing that I cannot find,
the lake where stones travel
searching lifetimes for the bottom.
Let silence come like animals
in the dark mountain night,
watchful yet unafraid, licking my body
with tenderness the way a mother bear
licks her cubs, less to clean them
than to give them strength.
Let the absent words dissolve
before they're formed
and the fret and strain of pulling
one sentence toward the next
slacken, until all that's left
is something wild and musical,
one note without speech.

Ethna McKiernan

In My Father's Voice

Remember that quote from James? Letters, in the New Testament?
It's a poor paraphrase, but something about the man who owns
two coats being a thief when the second man has none.

"But what's it for, except to give away,
to give it back? There's nine of you, a lot,
and my conscience veers left and right
each night, wondering whether
my small sums should go to you
or charity. When those voices come
I give it up to trust, to what we left
you, what was taught.

How I worry! That your children
won't collect Social Security, that
their children will be bankrupt.
Worry stalked me from the cradle, my father
dead at 35. Eleven, the oldest, I felt
the clocks seize that instant
but the worry kept on ticking.

God, am I wrong to want a new roof
for Áine, a safer car for Kate, college-help
for Sean, some family boost outside the palms
of the IRS *and* a shelter for the homeless
made of bricks and heat and beds,
real dollars, not just sentiment?

Dear Hearts, the same old lessons, I'm afraid,
from the same old man: feed the hungry.
Clothe the shivering. Fix your furnaces,
and pay off the Visa animal breathing
at your necks. But don't forget
the whole wide world alive and wanting,
the humming need of it. I love you,
do you know that? Give it back."

Ethna McKiernan

What do I write about? Well, *though I've written about Vietnam, Rodney Jones, the massacre at Waco, the workhouse in 19th century Ireland, I still couldn't characterize my poetry as necessarily political. Though I've written poems rooted in Ireland or the landscape of Lake Superior or ones referencing the Taco Bell on Lake Street, I can't say my poetry is primarily concerned with place, either. Neither is my vision grounded chiefly in the natural world.*

I'm drawn to persona, and have used it a lot, particularly in my first book, Caravan. *I've written from the voice of an Arctic explorer responsible for the death of a crew member; from the memory of an aging Florida widower recalling his New England past; from the delusional excitement of a manic-depressive; in parody, from the voice of a master poet experiencing writer's block; and from many other perspectives. Persona compels me because it is all about the imagination, and the entrance to the "other."*

Whether written in or out of persona, from the urge to bridge the political world with the personal world or the desire to explore the connection between place and identity, my main content concern has always been the meaning and complexity of human relationship. What matters more?

Alongside content, music matters: the song of poetry, the sound of it. And image, of course; the charged metaphor, the unexpected coupling, is essential.

Poetry doesn't occupy the altar in my life; mostly because it can't. I'm not an academic (nor do I want to be), so am not surrounded by literature, though I am surrounded by some good books in my book distribution business. But, as a small business-owner, and as a single parent, my time for writing is extremely limited.

I've written poems on napkins and matchbook covers, as well as in the rarified atmosphere of writing colonies or conferences. I'm grateful beyond belief for my times at those colonies and conferences, as those are the places where I shed obligation and do nothing but eat, breathe and sleep poetry. But I'm also glad I have a "real" life, a working community and family life to return to, with all its messy demands and complicated, glorious human needs.

(Photo by Vince Leo)

Robert Hedin is the author, translator, and editor of thirteen books of poetry and prose. Awards for his work include three NEA Arts Fellowships, a McKnight Artist Fellowship for Writers, the Loft Award of Distinction in Poetry, and many others. He has taught at Sheldon Jackson College, the Anchorage and Fairbanks campuses of the University of Alaska, St. Olaf College, the University of Minnesota, and Wake Forest University. Several years ago he returned to his native Red Wing, Minnesota, to found and direct the Anderson Center for Interdisciplinary Studies. From there he also edits *Great River Review*.

Turning Fifty

(For Carolyn)

So this is how it must've looked
that first day,
the gates to the garden
creaking shut, and both of them
just standing there
in the late afternoon light,
looking back, the rain
coming down hard,
the flowers closing up
their shutters, and the leaves,
the leaves already beginning to fall.

The Snow Country

(For Carolyn)

Up on Verstovia the snow country is silent tonight.
I can see it from our window,
A white sea whose tide flattens over the darkness.
This is where the animals must go—
The old foxes, the bears too slow to catch
The fall run of salmon, even the salmon themselves—
All brought together in the snow country of Verstovia.
This must be where the ravens turn to geese,
The weasels to wolves, where the rabbits turn to owls.
I wonder if birds even nest on that floating sea,
What hunters have forgotten their trails and sunk out of sight.
I wonder if the snow country is green underneath,
If there are forests and paths
And cabins with wood-burning stoves.
Or does it move down silently gyrating forever,
Glistening with the bones of animals and trappers,
Eggs that are cold and turning to stones.
I wonder if I should turn, tap, and even wake you.

Robert Hedin

Waiting for Trains at Col d'Aubisque

4 a.m. and rain since dark, rain dropping
From the slate roofs onto the stone walkway,
And all of us here—
The middle-aged mother and the child,
The three privates smoking
As only those going off
For good can smoke—
All of us standing at these windows,
Except the young boy out under the archway
Who has brought his father's coffin
Down out of these bare hills,
A small sheepherder's boy
Who doesn't care how old the night gets
Or how long this rain takes hold,
Only that his wool coat
Is folded neatly, and that his head rests
Over his father's shoulder,
For if this boy, this young dark-eyed Basque
From Col d'Aubisque
Whose skin will never again feel as wet
Or as wanted as it is
By all this rain,
If this small boy would talk
He would say we've stood all night
At these windows for nothing,
And that even if the morning comes
And we step out into the cold light,
Finding the world no better or worse
And ourselves still wanting
To be filled with its presence,
The words we've waited all night to say
We will have to turn into breath
And use to warm our hands.

Robert Hedin

Bells

(For M. L., killed in Viet Nam)

I remember it was 1965, the summer
    I was put in charge
        of the bells. Above me
and high up, they waited
    like thunderheads at the top
        of the First Presbyterian Church.
And so each Sunday I would pull,
    and down out of that dark
        ringing would fall,
like flecks of glittering mica,
    dead moths, flies, and the small
        luminous bones of bats.
But most of all it was dust.
    And all summer with the sun
        high in its arc,
and the heat building slowly
    by degrees, I rose, lifted
        by that long bell rope,
and, swinging there, would pull
    the dust down, like light,
        over the bowed and sleeping Bibles.

Goddard Hot Springs

When you lie in these sweating streams
You are lying in the breath of your ancestors,
The old pioneers who sat here in these pools
Mapping trails to the mother lode.
You feel a fog drift through your body,
A voice that is strangely familiar
And still has stories to tell.

Robert Hedin

The Old Liberators

Of all the people in the mornings at the mall,
It's the old liberators I like best,
Those veterans of the Bulge, Anzio, or Monte Cassino
I see lost in Automotive or back in Home Repair,
Bored among the paints and power tools.
Or the really old ones, the ones who are going fast,
Who keep dozing off in the little orchards
Of shade under the distant skylights.
All around, from one bright rack to another,
Their wives stride big as generals,
Their handbags bulging like ripe fruit.
They are almost all gone now,
And with them they are taking the flak
And fire storms, the names of the old bombing runs.
Each day a little more of their memory goes out,
Darkens the way a house darkens,
Its rooms quietly filling with evening,
Until nothing but the wind lifts the lace curtains,
The wind bearing through the empty rooms
The rich far-off scent of gardens
Where just now, this morning,
Light is falling on the wild philodendrons.

Robert Hedin

The main concerns of my poetry have always remained consistent: *home and home-ground, loss and reclamation, the integrity of everyday events, family life, our proper place in the natural world with all its seasonal turnings and yearly migrations, and the saving grace of the human imagination, our one true instrument of hope and reconciliation.*

Through poetry I attempt to articulate a landscape of conviction, a fundamental ground populated with shapes and contours, patterns and moments, that are common to us all. At some point, I believe, all stories become one story, a shared property where we are able to recover a certain communality of spirit. I approach each poem as a way of forging a compassionate pact with the world, retrieving in the process the great healing powers of the language.

Lucille Broderson was born in Willmar, Minnesota, and moved to St. Paul in her early adolescence. After earning a degree in literature and library science from the University of Minnesota, she resolved to become a fiction writer. "Five children came along," she says, "the last when I was forty. Though I kept at my L.C. Smith, not much happened. Then, suddenly, it seemed, I was in my sixties and found myself writing poetry."

Her poems have been published in *Poetry, TriQuarterly, Nimrod* and other literary journals. She has a manuscript, *My House Is Your House*, circulating for publication, and she also has completed a memoir.

White Milk at Daybreak

(After Paul Celan)

We wake on the hour of dread,
pray to the one who holds us, who carries us on her hip,
who could drop us over the void or lift us among the stars.
We pray and pray and feel within the worms
begin to crawl, the mold begin to form.
The cold, oh, the cold.
We creep beyond the haystack, dig deep in the fertile loam,
down down we sink, our home, our home.
We bow our heads before the plow,
whisper, "Cover us, cover us" over and over,
until all around, the meadowlarks, the daisies, the clover,
until all around the praises rise from the sea,
from the lakes, from the rivers, from the mountains,
the valleys, the plains. All around the notes
rise and rise and suddenly the clouds disperse.
The sun! Oh, white milk of the sun!

Lucille Broderson

Letter Never Sent

This letter is about me, the real me, the mother
you've never met. The one you invite to dinner
on Christmas or Easter is an imposter.
Or perhaps you already know.
But you'll act surprised
and hug me hard when next we meet. "Oh, no,"
you'll say, "you're not like that."

I did not have a father, that's true. He died.
"Oh, how she loved him, how she misses him!"
But I never missed him. I found another . . .
in the Elsie Dinsmore book.
He meant business, that father.
No! No! Do this! Do that!
And I did it all. Right. How pleased Mother was.
A child that is no trouble.

I grew up not pretty but pretty enough
and a young man wanted me.
He was as good a father as the book father.
He found the house, paid the bills, ordered the children,
loved me, he said, but I never believed.
He died. Too soon, of course, but he left me
"well enough off": my home, my car, my bankbook.
But I never loved him. Nor the man who followed him.

Then I woke and knew I hated the world,
the people in it, the books that stood every which way
on my shelves, the pages I'd written, the flowers on the table,
the wide snow-covered lake.

I never loved anything or anyone
but you, my children. Forgive me. It's true.

Lucille Broderson

Harvested Field

I walked in a moonless night
barely seeing the stubble around me . . .
I was looking for you.
You always said you'd meet me there.

Would you come if it were daylight
and everyone could say,
look, how faithful he is?
Would you come if the moon were shining
and you could see me, bright
as I was when we first met?

I sat on the old straw stack you plowed around,
hoping it would rot before the next planting.
I thought you'd be there with that old grin,
that you'd laugh, give me a little shove
and take me with you—wherever you've gone.

Although I heard the crackling behind me,
and knew your steps, you didn't come.

Now I walk the field in twilight,
the straw stack dank and crumbling.
Nettles sting and thistles cut my thighs.
In my throat an old crow nests.

Lucille Broderson

This Is Your Old Age, Lucy

When the sky is too blue,
when robins come in flocks
and fight in the birdbath.
When chrysanthemums freeze in the sun,
and geese are fat and float on the lake.
When the children jump from the bus
and run to someone else's door.

When your teeth find white bread tough
and apples cut into your gums,
when your face puckers and is small in the mirror
and you smile at the nose
you are finally willing to own.
When the man in your life fondles your breasts,
whispers lovely, lovely, and you are off
high in the bleachers observing.

Time when it's time and you hear
the train whistle and wonder where it's been
all these years, when, after forty winters,
you visit your mother's grave and think of her there,
boxed in the ground beneath you, her pink hands
still folded over the crepe de chine dress.

And you know,
you don't have to pack your suitcase,
check airline times and tickets.
Now it's just the crow's call, the far-off
rumble of a plane. It's tiny
crystals rubbing, silk strings touching.

Lucille Broderson

At Seventy-Eight

I hear in myself the lapping of water
—Milosz

But I do not hear, I yearn to hear,
the lapping of water near the boathouse.
No longer to dream of death, sinking slowly, quietly.
There's no end to the clouds in the distance,
racing toward me over the water,
painting the water black.

Oh fathers, why can't time move another way,
off through the fields, the snow-filled fields.

One hour comfortable, knowing the answers,
then the nagging way back in the brain.
The WATCH IT! and then
The roadblock, the great spiked logs in the road.

This morning, fog, dew on the windshield,
the windows. The lake an abyss,
the unknown, the unknowable.
Later, the sun and the lake wide open,
the red jagged rocks on the bottom
clearly visible and hardly a ripple.
At dusk the fog comes back.
Somewhere a child swings in the twilight.

It's time, I say, to board up the windows,
bolt the doors, drown the kittens
and feed the mice to the snake.
Time to haul off the rancid corn,
the dead cow and decaying horse,
to find the river and float away.

Somewhere a child climbs library steps, stands small,
expectant by the librarian's desk.
Shelves and shelves of books. Banks of high windows,
Sturdy little chairs in a half-circle.

Lucille Broderson

Live! snaps a crow from high in the cottonwood.
Wake! Wake!
And I do wake—
and know I've grown softer,
that the earth is not as hard as it was.
Today in these quiet woods, the sun shines,
clouds off over the lake,
clouds to every side
but here, the sun and the blue sky.

Somewhere, a mother at the dining room table,
books sprawled everywhere: Sunday's lesson.
The child sits on the floor and waits.

Lucille Broderson

I have learned from other poets *the value of reading lots of poetry then sitting down with my notebook, pen in hand, and letting come to me whatever wants to come. Picking and choosing later, sometimes much later, I discover a line here that seems to fit with two or three lines there. And just sitting with those lines, other lines come and ah, there's a poem, perhaps. Once but only once I remember a poem coming into my head out of nowhere. I was working around the house, in my bedroom actually, when something forced me to find pen and paper. True, I made some slight changes later, but the poem was basically there before I wrote it down. That really was a gift. But for me poems are always gifts. I do not work at them, except the revision, of course. But to receive them, I must be ready and quiet.*

Perhaps if one asked me what one needs most to bring the "muse" I'd say a quiet mind, a quiet place. A long walk alone perhaps, or sitting out in the yard or by a window. Squirrels out there, rabbits, birds. Wind, clouds. I've been extremely fortunate in being able to spend time each summer on the south shore of Lake Superior. How I love just to sit in the swing overlooking that magnificent lake. I love, too, to sit high on my porch here in the city, again overlooking a lake, a tiny lake, watching the Canadian geese, the mallards, the swallows in the air.

(Photo by Julie Anderson-Smith)

"I lack the colorful histories of some writers who have lived in New York or on the street," says **Tracy Youngblom,** "those who have accumulated lovers like loads of laundry, who have done drugs or time. For I am Minnesota born and bred, torn as I think many are between the country where I come from and the city where I have settled."

She has written poetry since fifth grade and her poems have appeared in a variety of literary journals including *Shenandoah, Loonfeather, Kansas Quarterly,* and *Briarcliff Review.* She has completed a first manuscript, *Growing Big,* and is working on a second while teaching at the University of St. Thomas.

Release

One Friday night I quickly give my love
an awkward public kiss, spin him
dizzily away, speed my children
off to their father, exchange polite
criticism and leave alone for the grocery,

where I become myself once more, childless
and cartless. My list a secret, I whistle
through aisles slinging looks
at the young men who dare to look
my way, who topple like a card house

under my gaze. I am exotic, elemental:
wind and light, promising nothing;
striding past the burdened, I hook
my cocoa and cream cheese
with one short but real fingernail.

I pass up grapes, carrots, anything
on sale, don't stop to look at toys,
balance what I want
in the bottom of my red basket, steal
glances at the families clustering

in frozen foods, children howling
like skittish coyotes. I shy away,
wide-eyed, aim for the express
checkout where Verla smiles past me
and I fit everything I need

in one small bag.

Tracy Youngblom

Sordid

Come, let's do something like that,
something base and unschooled,

like the word's meaning
before it was written down,

ascribed, applied, before it became
a precise formula or a sentence

for a crime—that's not what we want
from it, not *meanness* or *vileness*,

nor *filth* or *squalor*, no dirt, just the body
reaching past itself for definition,

for what it knows without being taught
and wants no language

to tell. Let's embody this word,
shape its meaning for a time

without vowels—the tongue's
difficult gestures—and capture

something unspeakable, details of which
are basic and often spare.

Joseph

My son plays Joseph in his pre-school pageant.
I believe he is typecast: sullen, confused
beside his Mary, who flaps her arms with the angels,
squeezes her floppy newborn, taken up with joy.

Their play ends too soon for my son to be redeemed,
to have his prophetic dream about fleeing to Egypt.
He never makes a decision of his own to settle
outside Bethlehem in the town where people would
later mock his son.

He spends his life there in the shadow of his wife's
blessedness, sanding wood so smooth it feels just
like the skin on the boy's back. He rubs it at night,
still oddly outside the light, an arm's length
from understanding the whole story.

My son gives me a print of his hand. It reminds me
that he will grow up, that it is hard to build
something that lasts, has meaning. On the card
he says, "I hope you get all your work done."

What does he say at the end of his life?
How much does he know?

Tracy Youngblom

On Sunday Morning the All-Men Worship Team Takes the Stage

Shoulder to shoulder on risers, three tiers
above the congregation, they lead
songs, clap and sway, unified, undifferentiated—
except for one hip, pink-shirted male
who crosses arms on his chest in rapt devotion,
one older man at the mike whose right knee buckles
and unbuckles in time to the music.
They could be the packed, persuaded
standing-room-only crowd at Pentecost,
or a tribunal of the disciples and all their male
cousins, but I see them as I saw
the man in my dream the other night:
He wouldn't hold me—or more correctly, held
me once, a wonderful melting, then withheld
the tenderness that was the center
of my need. He wanted me
to commit to him, marry him, follow
him (whatever women do in dreams)
for more of it. But without it
I could not move.

                All these men move,
are moved by the music. Toward
what? A hundred resurrections, they listen
to their own voices in pure tonal relation,
the triadic chords filling the room, hovering
near the ceiling where they cast
their God-burdened eyes. In their dreams
they get useful information—names of enemies,
important dates—power enough
to save themselves and the women
at their feet, of whom they ask nothing
great, only to pitch their voices in
at the foundation of the chord, to stitch healing
into the hems of their garments
and to bear, alone, the horror of love,
the burden of its insufficiency.

O Earthly Zion

From the crisp and final
mouth of the Almighty
gold streets roll forth;
and trees tall,
golden,
hard-edged and ripe and real
put down roots
to the crystal water
that shivers with its
own sufficiency
as it begets the fruit,
sweet and satisfying.
The leaves flutter themselves dry
on the wind that has now
no weight of grief in it.
They float radiantly outward
in the incessant brightness
of day and night,
carrying in their veins
the whole face of God.

Tracy Youngblom

Child's Drawing

Though he rests there quietly with all the others,
his black hair rises like smoke from a brush fire, curls
around his head like steel wool. His dark nose
claims the center of his face, as usual. When I scrape
his outline, a waxy trace remains. If I could take him
home, hold his face over a flame, I could change it,
melt it, tilt him into the trash and force a new identity
on him, almost like a birth. He could be colorful, finally,
and familiar. Children could look at him and recognize
their dreams. But I like the way his face looks up
from its position on the floor, how he's laid out flat,
quite comfortably, content with loss and hierarchy,
how he's been put there with the other clowns,
smiling because the whole world still emerges
from his smile, his open yet terrifying black mouth.

Whether I sensed in earlier Minnesota poets a shared sensibility, *a common field of experience, I responded to their descriptions of dailyness, the getting from here to there, the obligations and passions of life that I already recognized. My conservative beginnings tempered my rebellions; the farm saved me, but from what? There have been times I've regretted my relatively tame history, wished I had had a mother who valued sleep over church, who had dragged me from house to house or drank without remorse in front of me so I would have more to write about. But I don't. I have my simple tension, no more; my poems contain cows and bulls and farmers. And yet, I'm convinced the essence of poetry is not subject matter.*

What strikes me about good poems is that they command and control language. They SOUND good, before anything else, whether read silently or aloud, whether long or short, whether full of simple or complex words and phrases. There is such a thing as the right word or title, a captivating rhythm—sound in the service of meaning. And that meaning derives from the use of images and metaphors which, because they create pictures, require readers to think. We need metaphors to make connections between our chaotic lives and other lives or worlds. We need that light to go on, that understanding to dawn in order to survive the unknowable.

(Photo by Lynn Nankivil)

Though **Ken McCullough** was born in Staten Island, New York, spent most of his formative years in St. John's, Newfoundland, and finds Montana a continuing source of inspiration for his work, his move to Minnesota four years ago was deliberate, motivated in part by desire to be part of the active literary life of the state. He has received numerous awards for his poetry, including the Academy of American Poets Award, a NEA Fellowship, a Pablo Neruda Award, a Galway Kinnell Poetry Prize, the New Millenium Poetry Award, and the Capricorn Book Award. He is the author of several collections and most recently has been on tour with Cambodian poet concentration camp survivor U Sam Oeur, reading with him from their bilingual edition of U's collected poems, *Sacred Vows* (Coffee House, 1998). He is currently collaborating on U's autobiography and a translation of Whitman's *Song of Myself* into the Khmer language. He teaches at Winona State University.

Instructions

(For Shivani Arjuna)

Invite them in, these travellers
some with scars across their faces
others no more visible than blue smoke
whether their light flickers
or is so strong that you must turn away—
wash this one's feet, give that one
what you have, even if it's everything:
the days of love, the seconds, are not
numbered—what goes from you comes back
sevenfold. If you have to, run across
the surface of the water, but
for God's sake be quick about it.
When you're up to it, engage Death
in small talk, about the weather,
anything, then see if you can
trick him into turning inside out.

Visitation

(For Robert E. McCullough, 1908–1972)

On the beach, November, cold and alone, I lay there
looking up. I sensed you there and pushed to bring you
into focus. I started to cry and I could not cry. My
face was scrunched up like a baby's. It was trapped
inside me—a belt around my chest, a hand at my throat.
I called to you for help and you were there, above me
in the air, as you looked at maybe 42, your eyes dark
and glistening. I told you that I had been the way I was
with you: recalcitrant, bristling, itching for a brawl
because I was afraid of you, afraid of becoming you—
a shy countryboy who crumbled cornbread in his buttermilk,
who knew nothing but work from Day One, whose only vices
were being too honest, too generous for your own good.
I could breathe now, sighing, and my eyes were open.
I said I understood now, where it came from, the fear
and that I accepted you, now, and wanted you to be with me.
That we never talked, is done with—no guilt on either side.
I have not been able to accept what I am yet, and where
I came from. I want your help. I need you.
I held out my arms to you and you moved down
toward me steadily, and I could see your eyes as
you approached, fixed on mine—the reflections of me
lying there, confused, snotty-nosed helpless, and you
merged with me in a nimbus of light, and I wrapped my
arms around you as you came to me and I sobbed, deep and
long, and thanked you for letting me let you in, at last.

Edisto Island, S.C. 1978

Ken McCullough

Finishing Merrill Gilfillan's *Chokecherry Places* at the Cambodian Buddhist Temple, North Bronx

From my window, concrete ziggurat to the southeast,
walls of saffron and orange behind me, incense up the stairs,
calligraphy on posters, a happy embroidery.
I close the book, bundle against mid-March wind and
take to the streets, rambling, past secretive stream
under flyway distorted from below, klakkle of the El,
whoop and slap of milkcrate basketball, to small
Middle Eastern kitchen where I order spicy goat.
Boozy whitemen, of no known ancestry, come and go,
asking for caw-fee and cigarettes, see basmati rice
in heating tray and ask if it is Rice-a-Roni.
I think, on the other hand, of you, my friend
passing through the land, brushing away your footprints
as you go. Your words will not bring misguided pilgrims
to Cherry Creek, the Grand, the Mandan villages—
only others, like yourself, who leave no trace.

Ken McCullough

The Red and Black

(Late March, northern Wisconsin)

Along Highway 51, where the Bad River
wanders out of earshot, snow pelts my windshield
like huge white diatoms. I make out a road sign
which says **BEAR HABITAT.** Farther into this sea
of pummeling I sense I must get to the bottom.
Then I hear them calling: "Slow, slow . . .
turn off into the birches—park your van and leave it . . ."
I pull my hands up into my sleeves and listen—
"The snow will cover your tracks to our dens—
they cannot follow you. And when it stops you
will have to walk backwards the way you came here.
But how long a song it will be until tomorrow
and what your footprints will resemble is another
story altogether. We are waiting, brother."

Ken McCullough

Instructions

(For Galway McCullough)

Trace the backbone to where it disappears.
There, gentians suck the color from the sky.
You will see dancers, barely visible,
stumbling through the aspen as if drunk.
When you hear a crow's call rise like hunger,
traveling south, turn and sit. A fine pollen
will settle on your hair and shoulders.
Bring no weapons. Several bears will cross you—
even if a grizzly raises up and paws the air,
hold your ground. Breathe. Speak sharply.

It will be years before you get here.
The first time, be alone. If you need me
look over your shoulder, fifty paces back.
Call and I will see with you through your eyes.
And on this morning, this first morning,
you will sense love, the skin laid out for you
to put on for the rest of your life. It
will be blue—not the color of mountains
as the sunlight fades or of mourning,
but the color of feathers and of eyes
and of old ones who live beneath the snow.

You will hear the rhythms of an ocean
and your body will rise in slow spirals
up to the high place. From there you will see
the deep obsidian face of your past.
Deny the terrors. Let the quick lightning
writhe through you to set root in the center
of the earth. It will turn your blood to vapor.
You will smell, then, something like gardenias,
but far beyond its wildest echoes, so
clean you will weep tears of tourmaline.

You will know when to come down. Follow the
old road, the glad ice on the stream of light.
There are no dams here. The bark on your hands

will be white, my son, your eyes green moons.
Begin running ahead of time, into time,
no matter—you can dream now, forever.

Run, Late November

I thought it was silence, then the void
materialized, seven of them,
deer, etched and springing, a chorus,

fugue, glissando of deer singing
the white air to life. An antlered
trio cut from the frieze and turned

toward me, turned the white moon up
on the antlers of the grove.
I was running the road through the

graves when the night spilled its eyes
on my spine. Deer, seven, and three
veered to face me, one seasoned in

the moonlight. The sky filled with shapes
I knew—the plainsong of the dead
living with me all these years.

I've been living in Minnesota a scant four years, *and my connection with the state is restricted primarily to the part of the southeast known as the driftless (unglaciated) bioregion. I've traveled a great deal in my life and have always wanted to set down roots, though a large part of my sensibility has been that of an outsider, a drifter. Maybe it is no accident that I feel at home in this unique place—the goat prairies, the bluffs, the river towns, the rivers and streams, the climate, the people. While I continue to make forays further west, into South Dakota, Wyoming and Montana, I am starting to shift my spiritual focus to the area around Winona, and to derive sustenance from this place and its inhabitants—four-legged, two-legged, finned, winged. If I can learn to read and understand the text of this place, allow it to be my teacher, I will be happy. And if I can represent it in some meaningful way, I will be satisfied.*

I don't write one kind of poetry, am not content to speak with one voice. There is a bit of Coyote in me, and the Mimic facet of Coyote's nature has always appealed to me. Some of my poems are lyric, some narrative, some in tight and others in open forms. I am no stranger to the left margin, but am not bound by it. I love sonnets yet am fascinated by post-literate wrangling, though I don't understand much of it. My work does not lend itself to imitation, and, as a teacher, I do not encourage students to parrot what I do or have done. I guess I'd have to put myself in the Reform Party of poetry.

It's important to keep poetry operating outside the leaning tower of academia (as well as within). Yes, I love books, but song and recitation are where poetry live for me. I can't be bothered with much of what I come across in the magazines these days. For me, listening to singers at a Lakota sundance, in South Dakota, in the parched days of early August is at the heart of poetry. Listening to other languages in general. The way Leonard Cohen writes his songs—with intelligence, heart, anger, and compassion—the way Dylan is still able to surprise me with the quirky turns of his lyrics—both fuel my poetic engine. I prefer music, mystery and alchemy, with a large dose of humor.

Demythologizing and demystification be damned!

(Photo by Timothy Francisco)

Joyce Sutphen was born and raised on a farm in Stearns County that provided a panoramic view of fields spreading down to the Sauk River. The University of Minnesota lured her away from the farm and to a Ph.D. in literature. "Somewhere, despite all my uncertainty," she says, "I admitted to wanting to be a poet to a friend who also wrote poems. Hers were better than mine, I thought, but somehow she knew me for a poet as well. This is the honest truth: more than twenty-five years later, we shared a poetry prize at the University of Minnesota and we both published our first books of poetry when we were in our forties, right around the same time." Sutphen's first book, published by Beacon Press in 1995, was titled *Straight Out of View.*

Currently teaching at Gustavus Adolphus College, she has published poems in several literary journals and has won a number of awards, including the Eunice Tietjens Memorial Prize, given annually by *Poetry.* Her second book, *Coming Back to the Body,* was published this year by Holy Cow! Press in Duluth, which is also reissuing *Straight Out of View* in 2001.

Crossroads

The second half of my life will be black
to the white rind of the old and fading moon.
The second half of my life will be water
over the cracked floor of these desert years.
I will land on my feet this time,
knowing at least two languages and who
my friends are. I will dress for the
occasion, and my hair shall be
whatever color I please.
Everyone will go on celebrating the old
birthday, counting the years as usual,
but I will count myself new from this
inception, this imprint of my own desire.

The second half of my life will be swift,
past leaning fenceposts, a gravel shoulder,
asphalt tickets, the beckon of open road.
The second half of my life will be wide-eyed,
fingers sifting through fine sands,
arms loose at my sides, wandering feet.
There will be new dreams every night,
and the drapes will never be closed.
I will toss my string of keys into a deep
well and old letters into the grate.

The second half of my life will be ice
breaking up on the river, rain
soaking the fields, a hand
held out, a fire,
and smoke going
upward, always up.

Joyce Sutphen

From out the Cave

When you have been
at war with yourself
for so many years that
you have forgotten why,
when you have been driving
for hours and only
gradually begin to realize
that you have lost the way,
when you have cut
hastily into the fabric,
when you have signed
papers in distraction,
when it has been centuries
since you watched the sun set
or the rain fall, and the clouds,
drifting overhead, pass as flat
as anything on a postcard;
when, in the middle of these
everyday nightmares, you
understand that you could
wake up,
you could turn
and go back
to the last thing you
remember doing
with your whole heart:
that passionate kiss,
the brilliant drop of love
rolling along the tongue of a green leaf,
then you wake,
you stumble from your cave,
blinking in the sun,
naming every shadow
as it slips.

Joyce Sutphen

Launching into Space

At a certain stage, the engine drops
into the ocean and thrust carries the capsule
onward into space, where it is not dark
and star-studded as everyone always imagines,
but light as Milton's celestial fields, and fiery.

At a certain stage, the caterpillar disappears
into the gauzy wrap of its spun cocoon, and
hangs like an unfurled leaf from the branch.
Inside, the neat machinery of wing and antenna
is unfolding, the slow loom weaving its color.

A child, at a certain stage, will develop a sense
of distance and continuity. Until then, she will
think that the ball rolling behind the chair has
vanished. She will not expect you to return.
Later, she will see through walls to where you are.

And love, at a certain stage, will know exactly
when to look across the room and smile, when
to turn and say the words it almost would not
say, like bringing in an armful of wood,
something to keep the fire against the cold.

Joyce Sutphen

Comforts of the Sun

To someone else these fields would be exotic:
the small rows of corn stretching straight
as lines of notebook paper, curving slightly over
the rise of a hill; the thick green

of the oatfields, which I could predict
would turn into the flat gold of summer straw;
the curled alfalfa, slung like a jacket
over the shoulder of horizon.

To someone else, the small groves of trees
along the barbed-wire fence would look like
shrines to a distant god, little remnants
of woodland standing against the tilling hand.

Someone else would need to be told
that my footprints, in a hundred different
sizes, are etched under layers of gray
silt at the center of the farmyard,

that bits of my father's skin are plowed
into every acre. They would have
to be told how I know each tree,
each rock too heavy to lift.

Joyce Sutphen

My Father Comes to the City

Tonight his airplane comes in from the West,
and he rises from his seat, a suitcoat slung
over his arm. The flight attendant smiles
and says, "Have a nice visit," and he nods
as if he has done this all before,
as if his entire life hasn't been 170 acres
of corn and oats, as if a plow isn't dragging
behind him through the sand and clay,
as if his head isn't nestling in the warm
flank of a Holstein cow.

Only his hands tell the truth:
fingers thick as ropes, nails flat
and broken in the trough of endless chores.
He steps into the city warily, breathing
metal and exhaust, bewildered by the
stampede of humanity circling around him.
I want to ask him something familiar,
something about tractors and wagons,
but he is taken by the neon night,
crossing carefully against the light.

Joyce Sutphen

Casino

My mind is shuffling its deck tonight,
slipping one card over another,
letting them fall together at the corners.
The random hand of memory
is dealing from the bottom of the pack.

First: a bearded man emptying
the dragon kiln, then a woman
whistling, her face turned away
as she opens the oven. Next:
a big cat, six toes on each paw,
climbing up the yardpole. Last:
a pair of workhorses circling a tree
until they grind themselves to dust.

There is no one home in the world
tonight. Everyone is out of range.
The cradles are empty, the boughs
broken down. Trees go helter-skelter
and the wheel is creaking on its shaft.
Hit me, I say to the dealer. Hit me again.

My father used to make up little poems that he would tell me when we were milking cows or up in the hay-barn, throwing hay down for the night. He'd say, "Here we are in the dark—what a lark! Hope we don't see a shark!" or "I used to want to be a cowboy, but now I really am a cowboy," and then he'd laugh. You can imagine that I didn't see much connection between my father's fanciful brand of rhyming (a cross between Ogden Nash and Bob Dylan) and the poetry I swooned over in high school (Chaucer, Shakespeare, Emily Dickenson). I loved the way the sounds of words bumped up against each other, love the rhythms of words in lines and (sometimes now) in rhymes.

 I have collections of things poets have said about poetry: How when you read something and feel that the top of your head is taken off, that is poetry; how poetry is the thing that gives us the worlds we turn to (and desperately need) without knowing for certain whether or not they are there—the "supreme fictions," or how it's like walking that has started dancing. I believe too, that "It is difficult/to get the news from poems/ yet men die miserably every day/for lack/of what is found there."

 Finishing a poem that I like makes that day a success, no matter what other things failed or fell by the wayside. When I am working on a poem—really working on it—hours can go by and I stay sitting in the same place moving words, deleting lines, changing line breaks, adding a stanza, changing a comma. I don't notice that my coffee is cold, that I haven't had anything to eat, that my shoulders are stiff—I am absorbed in the making of this thing called a poem, the thing I am reading over and over to myself until it comes out right, until it says what I now know I wanted to say. If I could walk back in time, I would stop into my high school guidance office, and I would say: poet—that's what I would like to be.

(Photo by Annie Lehrke)

"I identify with the Midwest," says **Philip Dacey,** having been born and raised in St. Louis, Missouri, "and I've been a resident of Minnesota for thirty years, though I am not, as a rule, for better or worse, a writer who celebrates his or her place." Dacey has spent most of his career at the Minnesota State University in Marshall, where he continues to teach part-time. His five earlier books are complemented by two new recent collections of poetry, *The Deathbed Playboy* (Eastern Washington University Press, 1999) and *The Paramour of the Moving Air* (Quarterly Review of Literature, 1999).

She Writes Offering to Buy for Her Son, in Minnesota, an Electric Blanket

I may be eightysome years old but I know
no woman in her right mind wants to screw
in a house whose temperature is kept so low
the cats sneeze all day and her hands turn blue.
What you and Suzie Q. do with yourselves
under covers a foot deep—trust me—only passes
for love: it's premature burial. Or else
you toss the damned things off and freeze your asses.
So for her sake if not yours, let me buy you
a good electric blanket for your igloo.
I didn't raise an idiot, don't act like one.
I deserve a completely defrosted son.
And heat soothes old bones better than a pill.
You don't have such things, Mr. Young? You will.

Badlands Love

He asks her, "Where'd you like to do it you haven't yet?"

Out in the Badlands, bent back over a rock
at night just after a summer rainstorm has passed.
A few drops are still falling, cold on my breasts
as you arch up and the distant lightning crackles

and the thunder rolling away seems an echo
of our low sounds. With what feels like the same
hardness above and below me, I'll come and come
and you won't even have to whisper fuck

in my ear, thanks to this landscape I so love
I like to think that lit by flashes we're
just one more strange formation here,

forked, a natural wonder. Who wouldn't believe
tomorrow there'll be burn marks where we stood?
Dakota ghosts know what's bad is the sweetest good.

Philip Dacey

Nomen, Numen

Tuncks is a good name, Gerard Manley Tuncks.
  —GMH from his *Journals*

I am haplessly hopelessly Hopkins.
What is a Hopkins? A series of little
Hops. Leaplets. Nothing sustained. Nothing whole.
Hobbled-kind. Hare-minded. What begins
Well ends one length away. Half-happens.
A plan, hope-full, for poem, or more, hurries to a fall.
A man breathes in, puffed, breathes out, flat. That's all.
My name (help!) spells me out: what's whole? my sins.

Ah, but Tuncks. Tuncks. I would give such thanks
To be so named. Sound sound manly single.
Blow well-aimed at a mark; thought an arrow thinks.
Thunk. Thud. Straight for God. Good. Nothing will
Do but dead center, the heart of the Triangle
's Word, Holy Name no silence (sh!) outflanks.

Philip Dacey

Counsel to the President

After the heart bypass and before the trial of Robert Altman, Clark Clifford occupied himself by reading the collected poems of W. B. Yeats.
—Michael R. Beschloss

A sudden blow, the indictment beating still
against my fibrillating heart, that thrilled
so when each year I'd pocket a cool mill.

No greasy fingers fumbled in my till,
but manicured, which set the tone for all
the lawyers who followed me, their courtly slouch

toward Washington to be born this time rich,
a terrible beauty draining brains deep
into Potomac corridors beyond reach,

sacrifice of the provinces' prime crop.
Missouri, for instance. I would arise and go
back home to ride with Truman's whistlestop,

like swans forever young at Coole, or throw
the poker game Sir Winnie thought he won
enroute to Fulton for the Iron Curtain speech.

O sage Cuchulain and sage Acheson,
my guardian warriors, one hot and one cold,
tell me I'm not changed utterly, but simply old,

that my good name which ever brightly shone
persuades hearts still, as if it were Maud Gonne.
But spirits fade at the ring of a phone—

it's Lady Bird or Jackie just saying hello.
At the club, few handshakes, and I eat alone.
Who goes with Fergus or with Clifford now?

My famous gesture—the judicious press
of fingertips together topped by my advice,
what journalists called "Clifford's wisdom-tent"—

Philip Dacey

feels like the merest arrangement of small bones.
Nothing can be whole that has not been rent:
loopholes were my life, through which now dolphins

plunge, ecstatic as their tails mock my hopes
for First American, whose chairmanship
proved I kept only a rag-and-bone shop.

How can you tell a banker from his bank?
Turning and turning in the widening hunt
for smoking paper trails, the banshee-accountants

can so far claim to have transformed my swank
hair—thick, waved, distinguished, a blinding mane
that once made women, and investors, swoon,

as silver as the apples of the moon—
into thin, loose strands as white as a ghost
that lifts and falls like Connemara mist.

Yeats dreamed angels copulated to breed
light; I dreamed money fucked itself for no
reason and spawned a stain like clouded blood.

The consummate insider thrust outside,
I push my floor's number and rise into
the vaulted sky of a New York apartment.

This is my tower at Ballylee. From here,
I see Central Park and Ireland's wild shore,
where a fisherman casts his long lament.

Philip Dacey

Walt Whitman's Answering Service

Who calls here,
hankering, gross, mystical, nude?

Did you expect to find me at home?
Then you do not know me.
I am never at home.
I am always on the road.
All roads lead to the telephone;
wherever you go, on or off
the road, a telephone wire
sings beside you.

I knew you would call.
Everyone does,
in his or her own way.
All the wrong numbers you dial
are meant for me,
are the attempts of your better self
to make the call
you are afraid to make.

If you would have me know who you are,
leave no name or number,
simply give to this line
the mist of your breath
and I will recognize you.

I will call you back
unless you wait by the phone
for me to call you back.
Be confident, but be warned:
my voice could be disguised
as anything, anything.

If you love me,
if you truly wish to get through to me,
you will hang up
at the sound of the tone
and dial your own number.
If the line is busy
or no one answers,

Philip Dacey

consider yourself lucky,
you can always call again.
If the line is out of order,
remember, you are the only repairman.
If the line has been disconnected,
remember, the only phone company
is yourself.

No method, as the Chinese say, *is the best method. Which means, All methods when appropriate. I believe in options: a large palette, a wide and deep toolbox. Thus in the eighties, through* Strong Measures *I took (with help from Dave Jauss) a swing at Bly, Kinnell, & co., their demagoguery vis-à-vis fixed form, whereas in the nineties, I've found myself warring at the other end of the spectrum with Jarman, Mason, & co., their demagoguery as New Formalists. Exclusivists, all of them. Me for inclusivism.*

Though I've been a resident of Minnesota for thirty years, I've travelled widely, here and abroad, and written more about Hopkins in Dublin and Whitman in New Jersey than about me anywhere. I feel like a hovering bird, cruising the landscape, never settling down anywhere. The exception is the last ten years, when I've been living on an acre of land in the country, in a valley near a state park. Beautiful house in a beautiful spot; my closest next door neighbors four horses in a pasture. Quite a few poems reflect that recent decade's experience, though they're still in the vast minority of those I write.

I suppose the above two paragraphs dovetail thusly: my detachment from a particular method—some template with which one can immediately tell the good guys from the bad guys—is echoed in my detachment from a particular place. Shouldn't we always have our bags packed and be ready to move on from whatever to whatever?

In summary, maybe I'm more of a plains writer than I think. I'm aware of that horizon over yonder, calling me away.

Philip Dacey

(Photo by Steve Krum)

"My life as a Minnesotan is my life as a writer," says **Mary Kay Rummel.** "The one occasion when I seriously considered moving to another state, I was held here by my awareness of the support of the literary community and the importance of this place to my writing." In addition to work published in literary magazines, she has had three books of poetry published: *This Body She's Entered* (New Rivers Press, 1989), *The Long Road into North* (Juniper Press, 1998), and *Green Journey, Red Bird* (forthcoming from Loonfeather Press). She has also co-authored *Teachers' Reading/Teachers' Lives* (SUNY Press) and co-edited an anthology, *American Voices: Webs of Diversity* (Merrill). She teaches at the University of Minnesota in Duluth and lives in Fridley, Minnesota.

Reading

There was a sound of geese from the bay
of geese or harmonica
and the way the sun idled
over the lake's cloud wall
revealing hills burning
was the way the geese advanced
dragging their phrases
across the water not on wind
but on memory
and that is why white rabbits
startled from their daytime places
beneath bushes and under cars
are the words in a child's book.

Mary Kay Rummel

Sonata

I sit in my car in the parking lot
listening to the end of an adagio
and watch a man and a woman
put groceries away.
He bends to the shopping cart,
plucks paper bags up, puts them in her arms.
She places each carefully in the trunk.
Maybe it's the Brahms
but I see they make music:
he is a pianist, his fingers
a ululation, perfectly tuned to take
and let go; she is a cellist, arms bowing
across the twilight where leaves minuet.

He throws the keys to her
over the roof of the battered Toyota.
Inside she pulls up the door lock for him.
My eyes follow their kiss, their drive away.

Adagio, adagio, adagio.
Let it go slow:
let me live each movement
through to its end,
let me know I will never
see this again,
or this, or this,
let me hear it as music
the cadence, the rhythm
that shimmers
over and over
between us
every and other.

Mary Kay Rummel

In the Night Kitchen

When I live in the north alone
I wake in the early morning
and see in the brittle sky three moons
aligned, moons within the moon, spring moon
with bright patina a crystal reflecting light, winter
moon like old aluminum tarnished bottom of a pan,
pale fragment morning moon simply fading.
My life hangs there like cookware.

The woman who shimmered is gone.
In the tarnished face, nicked and scratched
by love, I see my own diminishment, one who
is and is not fading. I wonder if it could
be the other way, a moving from pale to dull
to shining, the shimmering ahead not behind
the body inside the body wild
polished by the miraculous dark.

Mary Kay Rummel

Burgundy Trillium

Head hangs too heavy for its stalk

three petals curled back into red-lined leaves
      reveal the acidic yellow, furred center

stem springs from three lower leaves
      a storyteller's dream

A woman walking picked one:
she pulled one petal and a child appeared with a question
      she pulled another and a young woman appeared, an answer
           pulled the last and an old woman came just in time

Not related to tripalium, the Roman torture thing
      that birthed travail and from that travel
           no, that's another story

Related to trio, the clovered trinity
      to trill, warbling and wind gashed
           and to the wine red of unicorn tapestries

A trinity of women there.
All the same woman:
    one sews
        one looks in a mirror
           one puts away her jewels.

Mary Kay Rummel

Medieval Herbal

Let the man drink out of a church bell
Yarrow lupine lichen betony
Let him sing while he drinks
Beati Immaculati

Let the woman remain a virgin
Until twenty-seven or eight
Thus she will find her true origin
Let her drink fennel against folly

In her thirties when she is dry
She should climb the Tor of St. Catherine
Pick purple monkshood, beware the poison
In the root, but taste true passion

For heartache give brambles
Pound the leaves, lay them over the breast
Of both male and female

At forty she will explode with pleasure
Give her wild marjoram for a sore head
The spirit plant parsley in good measure
For the lunatic gentian and fennel

The herb of greatest future is marigold
If it be put in a church where the woman sits
Who has broken her matrimony
It will not let her leave until desire is put away

This has been proven true

At fifty the body will quiet
But she is not ready to stop
Rosemary cures impotence
For men and women both

Blessed be carnations for they
Shall be called the flowers of god
Grow pansies, love's casualty

Mary Kay Rummel

Spider webs brush against her face
After rain she notices the fuzziness
Of late summer leaves

Finds it on her own skin
The hairs catch water, hold it
Now she is like rue

Rain and sun reach all of her

Mary Kay Rummel

September 23, 1973 was the day that Pablo Neruda died. His death, and the events surrounding it changed my life, my view of language and the way I see and feel about my country. Allende was assassinated; the military took over in Chile, with the assistance of the United States. I found myself at a memorial service for Neruda in Minneapolis, led by Robert Bly and Meridel LeSueur. I began to understand poetry as a revolutionary act and began reading women poets who lived this belief, like Neruda, integrating belief, life and writing.

I have shared the writing lives of these women over the years so that when they are successful I feel a part of it. As I write this I realize how important the particularity of this place is for me. I travel to other places and I am inspired to write by those travels, but my poetry is written in Minnesota and its best audience is here.

For me poetry has always been an action by which I both come to self-knowledge and affirm that discovery through language. Because I came from a background of silence, it has been a way of breaking that silence. Poetry has always been tied to feeling and personal perception and has been a saving gift for me in my life. It has loosened the tongue, prophecy, speaking out.

Mary Kay Rummel

(Photo by Tony Hainault)

Opportunity took **Greg Hewett** from New York to California, to Japan and Scandinavia, and, finally, here to Minnesota. "I've found a place to settle," he says. "I live in Saint Paul and work at Carleton College in Northfield. I wander scraps of the Old North Woods on foot, on skis, by snowshoes. I have my favorite haunts in the Cities—the coffee's good, the plays are great."

Hewett's first book of poems, *To Collect the Flesh,* won the New Rivers Minnesota Voices competition in 1996, and his second, *Red Suburb,* will be published by Coffee House Press. His work has appeared in many publications, and he has been the recipient of two Fulbright fellowships and a Minnesota State Arts Board Grant.

Memorial Fountain

Like pale seals,
boys haul themselves from the deep

marble basin where they're forbidden,
and sprawl on laps of gods and heroes.

They squint in the colossal sun,
shiver in winter's fragments,

take shelter among columns
in a mandala of golden light.

They rub their blue legs together and laugh
hard at each other's shriveled scrotums.

Like soldiers they share damp smokes
and swig from the same bottle.

I move over the border
of tulips rippling like a ring of fire,

beyond the plaza, into a grove
of budding oaks, the understorey

overflowing with rhododendron.
In opalescent light men move

along sinuous paths, hear the archaic
laughter, and we remember

swimming in the fountain not caring
what lay beyond the sun-hammered paving.

Greg Hewett

Turtle Music

I dream my grandmother phosphorescent,
braids and arms white with fire; ragged star,
she floats through salt and shale chambers
in the river deep underground.

I hear my grandmother's dark chant echo
in sunlight, in the open air, echo
off the high shale walls of the gorge, echo
with the endless songs of water woven in the one.

I see my grandmother rise under the falls,
rise and circle with the turtle
whose shell vibrates with music,
the music of water and shale.

I watch my grandmother's flint-black eyes
behind the changing screen of water,
and I am afraid because I keep no spirit,
afraid because I do not believe in ghosts,

afraid of secrets from the cliffs and underground,
afraid because in my rock-n-roll childhood
I never kept the promise
to learn her song, the one, the turtle song,

and now I am so lost.

The Distance to Birth

Sometimes I find myself
surprised over my own passing

youth like I've just uncovered
the gold face of some boy

pharaoh in the sand.
Through dust orbiting

in a tunnel of sunlight I look
out on the park at a boy

as ancient as men get
and see he's unshaken

by the news. He surely knew
he was old when I was born,

he knows men now petrified
in busts, and those who simply died

unnoticed, he knows
October roses well,

how their dark perfumes
color the rising breeze,

and he knows why leaves
red as dawn circle him

as he progresses toward a shadow
blue and certain as the distance to birth.

Greg Hewett

Hymn of 1978, the Last Word

Knowing how she used the word gay
in the old-fashioned way,
I told her I was homosexual,
something clinical.

I didn't understand the word
had entered the lexicon
after she was born,
too late to enter

her backwoods vernacular,
and I was too modern to relate
to her biblical sodomite,
so beside her gray bed I sat

looking into blind eyes
as I touched her damp forehead
and we found ourselves a silence
too strong for last words.

Greg Hewett

Two Sons of the King of Delhi Hanged, 1857

In the shiny new museum of modern art shaped like a sun temple
    or camera,
        we file past a daguerreotype
of dead princes from a dead kingdom and a dead century, unmoved

or moved as we are by other images in the gallery, for instance
of Lincoln's killers, one female, the mother of one of the others hanged
        in a row on the deck of a ship in the Potomac,

or the police photo of a concierge in a heap of bloody crinoline,
garroted in a narrow flat in Paris not long after the time of Poe,

as much as we are moved or unmoved by the Palestinian shot dead
        on the West Bank yesterday that we saw
on the morning news, or by shepherds' wells more than one hundred
    feet deep,

represented by black circles on the t.v. screen, in a hard-looking land
        where we don't know
how many Afghanis threw some hundreds of other Afghanis down alive
    and grenades after them just in case, as much as we are

moved or unmoved by the paper at breakfast showing a girl's bloody
    underwear
        in black-and-white found in a locker in Minnesota,
or by glossy magazine pictures of holiday crowds outside a luxury
    department store
        in London, bleeding, bits of glass stuck in their faces,

and moved or unmoved in this new museum, I want to stay
with the two boys, the princes, the sons of the King of Delhi captured

in exacting daguerreotype, executed
more than a hundred and forty years ago now, for,
    as the caption says, murdering several British

colonialists, and unmoved or moved
I want to know how many were murdered, I want to stay

because the mourning or jeering crowd, if there was any,
is already dispersed, and the landscape has not a tree or frond, flower or
    even weed,

Greg Hewett

and their thin, beautiful bodies just hang there with no explanation
as to why the one boy is mostly undressed, while the other wears
    a gauzy tunic and ballooning trousers,

even though they are both turbaned and both sons
of the King of Delhi hanged, and we aren't told about justice,
    about good or evil, just the image,

taken in a place bleak as a minimalist stage set, and moved
or unmoved, I have to know where the British are,
    and why only a handful of Indian men left watching,

and why no mother mourning two sons, and only
one old man looks moved, the rest unmoved, and of course the
    photographer remains

anonymous, standing where we stand, moved
or unmoved, and the executioners too.

I've never been sculpted in butter at the State Fair, *often feel outside Garrison Keillor's inside Minnesota jokes, and Jesse the Body's a big so-what to me, but still I feel attached to this Western Great Lakes State I moved to a decade ago. Maybe it's the watery connection to the shores of Ontario and Erie of my upstate New York childhood? Maybe it's the Great Lakes dialect we share? In any case, I represent a new-old kind of American and Minnesotan, that is, the migrant.*

Poetry will always be "making" for me, as it was for the Greeks. I know and respect various traditions of poetry, and yet I'm old-fashioned enough to be an early Modernist with my desire to "make it new." Poetry's got to sound like it comes from the turn-of-the-millennium without sounding faddish. Kant had it right when he said art is subjective, but has a subjectivity approximating the universal. This is old-fashioned, too. Retrograde. But there are flickers of the universal out there, I know. It's in Pope's salon and it's in African American spirituals; it's in Dickinson's House of Possibility and it's in Native American song. It's definitely in Langston Hughes and in Rimbaud. I teach literature and I know Chaucer, Marlowe and Shakespeare didn't write polite lines all of the time. Neither did Shelley or Byron. Certainly not Whitman and H.D. And so on. So I am wary of the politeness of so much poetry today. It's so dry and overly meditative. Or else it's obscure. Or, worse yet, it's sentimental, wallowing in how one ought to feel, not leaping into the clarity of what one feels. I don't go for a lot of the sensationalistic spoken-word poets, but I admire the life that flows there. In short, I look for a poetry that weds the spoken and written traditions, that is both sensual and intellectual, that has emotion but remembers that those emotions need form. Above all, there's got to be music (not to be confused with mellifluousness), and that music's got to sing to us in the here and now.

(Photo by Mary Lieberman)

Born and reared in the Midwest, **Claire van Breemen Downes** moved to Minnesota in 1969, when her husband accepted a professorship at St. Cloud State University. For years, with five children at home, she nurtured her family, her own teaching career at St. Cloud State, and her writing life. "Now," she says, "the children are grown and gone; Alan and I are both retired from teaching at SCSU; and we have never been so busy."

She has published several poems and stories in literary journals, and her creative prose is included in *Twenty-Six Minnesota Writers* (Nodin Press, 1995).

Mulberry Creek

I had forgotten mulberries:
    their squish underfoot,
    their pale stain in the bird-droppings on the shed roof;
    the old tree, ragged as a poor relation;
    and my sister, wearing my brother's pants,
        walking the roof of the shed,
        syrup bucket tied to her waist,
        picking what she could reach.

The berries themselves are bland, almost furry,
    with a core like pipe-cleaner—
    like biting down on a caterpillar, I used to think.
A good pie fruit, though, with a generous dash of lemon.
    Fit for company, steaming-fresh.

And the talk went back and forth
    across the cloth (cotton damask, worn thin,
    proudly white, crisply pressed):
Talk of the size of grasshoppers
    (Did they really eat the hoe handles?)
Rumors of the dust-storms farther west
(Dark skeletons of deserted farms shadowed us, were gone.)
Someone had seen signs hoboes had used
our fireplace in the woods. Too near the railroad, that was it.

Life in the cities must be even worse.
    but will there be a harvest this year?
A sin to plow under all those crops
    while people starved. God punishes.

Those were the old times.
Your children may not like the berries much.

Claire van Breemen Downes

Love Song at Evening

Rest in the silver shadows a while,
Where leaves make lace of the sun's last rays,
Nor look to the road and the dust-gold haze
That covers tomorrow's urgent mile.

Rest in the silver shadows with me.
Forget that the day has blazed and died
In dusty triumph, small dreams denied.
Forget tomorrow. Forgetting, see

We rest at last, love. Rest we must.
Others inherit the dream, the dust.

Postscript to an Old Myth

The earth was never tender to her young.
She shrugged them off in earthquakes, froze them out,
swept down in floods, or shriveled life with drought,
sent cyclones scything trees to which men clung.
She sometimes flicked a random, flaming tongue
of lava from a bursting mountain-spout,
smiling the while, lest anyone should doubt
that life and death from one same source are sprung.

We call her mother. Though she gave us birth,
she is a senseless mass of rock and mud.
She knows us not, though we make her complete.
Cling to each other. Ask not from the earth
forethought and kindness. Only flesh and blood
consciously walk through this uncertain street.

Golden Time

(Pantoum)

In this sweet, radiant summer of our life,
      The honey oozes golden from the comb.
The grain that greened so early now is ripe.
      Honey and harvest we bear gladly home.

The honey oozes golden from the comb,
      Amber to liven all our winter bread.
Honey and harvest we bear gladly home,
      Our sunlight for the graying months ahead,

Amber to liven all our winter bread.
      Shared fragrance nourishes our daily song,
Our sunlight for the graying months ahead,
      Brightness and comfort, though the dark seems long.

Shared fragrance nourishes our daily song
      In this sweet, radiant summer of our life.
Brightness and comfort. Though the dark seems long,
      The grain that greened so early now is ripe.

Claire van Breemen Downes

A Double Sonnet in Honor of My Hundred-and-Twentieth Birthday

If still the eagles soar beyond the trees
that edge the water where the last ice cracks
and jostles as the river shrugs and frees
itself of winter; if the fragile wax
of bloodroot hides deep in spring's moist-moss wood,
and columbine comes venturing in June;
if doe and fawn may stand where once they stood
when we could watch, that evening all in tune;
if birches still may shimmer forth in green
and lilacs keep their old familiar scent—
if these remain, then I may sleep serene,
nor wake to wonder where our moment went.
Canary tokens, these, of life and breath—
their total is a greater sum than death.

If now your cities, hived and busy, gleam
clean-swept and sunlit, joyous and secure,
as alabaster as the patriot's dream,
as radiant, undimmed, as angel-pure—
where no child cries unhushed, unloved, unfed;
no women hide their bruises and are shamed;
where roses are as daily as the bread,
and laughter rises, and no one is blamed;
where parks are April-green and flower-bright,
where none will ever know the bitter rain
of fire bombs or missiles, or the sight
of wounded bodies or the sound of pain—
then I shall have no promises to keep
and, resting, I shall smile soft in my sleep.

Claire van Breemen Downes

Over the past thirty-some years, I have taken part in the Minnesota writing community. For me, A View from the Loft *and* Minnesota Literature *are essential reading. I was part of a writing group here in St. Cloud for some years. As it ceased to function, I became involved in the formation of Heartland Poets in Brainerd. I am an advocate of such small support/critique groups, for there, among trusted friends, one can try new ventures safely. The right small group encourages risk-taking.*

Poetry is risk-taking, and risk-taking has results, positive and otherwise. When we use poetry to address painful concerns—death and illness, poverty and injustice—the atmosphere changes about us. (Once I asked of Lady Godiva, "When you rode through Coventry, was it this cold?" She didn't answer.)

Sometimes I think of poetry as akin to research writing, which I taught for years. Creative research is the laying side by side of ideas which had never met before, thereby creating a new vision. A poem, too, should introduce concepts to each other, let them illumine each other, let them—if necessary—fight it out, emerging new and one.

Debating whether authentic poetry is embodied solely in fixed form or in free verse seems irrelevant. Rhyme and meter can add useful dimensions to the idea of the poem or, unskillfully used, can destroy it. A complex traditional form can sharpen the challenge of presenting an idea—or the form can dominate and distort the poem. (The first question the poet should ask upon completion is "Have I sacrificed the poem to the form?") Free verse can present the poem vividly and urgently—or it can bury it under sloppy, prosy trivia. The poetic ear and poetic integrity of the writer must remain on duty, no matter what the form chosen for writing.

233

(Photo by David Grothe)

Margaret Hasse is a poet, educator, and arts consultant with a distinguished history of service to the Minnesota arts community. Originally from South Dakota, she moved to the Twin Cities after graduating from Stanford University in 1973. Her publications include *Stars Above, Stars Below* (New Rivers Press, 1984) and *In a Sheep's Eye, Darling* (Milkweed Editions, 1988). She has received several poetry fellowships, and currently is at work on a third book with a working title, *Strangers and Kin*.

Grave

. . . in the black of desire we rock and grunt and shine.
—**Denise Levertov**

At fifty, I wake in the orphanage
of my life, my parents' ashes buried
three decades ago in a bluff view
cemetery which looks out on the hills
of Nebraska, blue in the distance.
I once sat on the cold granite stones
recently chiseled with the names I love
beside a man I had not yet touched.
We watched the sun set, took off
our clothes and made love
with the pale ghosts of each other
on the grave of my family.

He first massaged the curved bones
in my pelvis, the ribs beneath my breasts
as if to be sure my skeleton
could bear his weight before we rolled
slowly like dogs on the carcass of death.
I feel his fingers on me now moving
rung by rung down the ladder of my backbone
toward the marl of my origins,
my sadness and sex.
A light joy talcs my body as if
I were abandoned as a child, then
fell into good hands.

Margaret Hasse

Bean Fields

They labor along the straight lines of their
parallel rows, the farm boy, the town girl
earning an hourly wage for her college fund,
weeding, staying even with each other,
learning they like each other's smell.

He has the slight acrid burn of green leaves.
She, catnip—residue of shampoo—
her hair streaked shades of brown
like the fizzy tassels at the top of corn.
His Tom body yowls in the backyard

of his brain that he wants that minty weed.
She, too, longs for the end of the row
when they will sit in the bed of the dirty truck
against warm rubber tires, drink
lemonade with tongues so keen

you could map the exact spot where
the sugar of desire does its dream business,
where the lemon pulp—call it
her education plan, his religious training—
persists in its tart denial.

A bean in its ripe casing hangs on a stem,
three fuzzy lumps in its throat. One for the boy,
one for the girl, and one for how the hinge
of what might happen to us swings slightly,
opening here, closing there.

Margaret Hasse

A Favorite Dessert, Lips

A young couple, cautioned
to stay above the neckline, leaves small favors
below, hickies decorating the throat.

They kiss where the sun doesn't shine,
or the moon either, deep inside.
To the flavor of the voice.
To the mushroomy scent.

The lungs, liver, heart,
all organs and the internal time-keepers, pace-makers,
pituitary glands, isthmuses, islands,
red seas, bridges, plants, nebulae:

everything alive waits to be eaten.

Cleaning the mouth of the other,
teeth clacking together like silverware
in their velvet drawers,
they murmur: "I like the way you do that.
I like you. It feels so good, oh god,
I want to die."

Margaret Hasse

Lilacs in the Ditch

Disappointed when the lilacs
rusted so quickly this spring,
we start to see ourselves,
my friend and I, as women
of gray streaked hair
with whom the old butcher
feels free to flirt.

Driving tired into the cooler
north of Minnesota, we
discover masses of purple lilac
just beginning to bloom
like rain clouds roiling up
the sleeve of the horizon.

The bushes call us from our
car, and we stand in the ditch,
our shoes wet with forgiving
dew, and break big pieces
of blossom in a rough
hungry way, laying the stolen
flowers on newspapers
in the backseat—like shards
of lavender stars—or sparklers
which we used as children
to write our names in the dark.

Margaret Hasse

Marking Him

Does my little son miss the smell
of his first mother? I wonder
as the mew of his mouth
opens toward a plastic bottle
which is not her breast.

In her good-bye letter to him
sealed in his album
with a birth certificate which now
lists my name as Mother,

his first mother writes
she nursed him briefly
after he emerged into
the second room of his
world.

        I think of milk volcanic
and insistent, answering
the newborn's gigantic hunger,
a primal agreement between
generosity and greed.

Sometimes
I press my nose
to the glass of that place
where a woman and my child
belong to each other;
I cannot imagine coming
between them.

Sudden new mother,
I bury my nose deep into
his skull cap of ringlets,
his starry cheesiness,
want to lick him all over
with a cow's terry-cloth tongue,
to taste and mark him as mine

Margaret Hasse

so if the other mother returns,
she will repeat the doe rabbit's
refusal of the kit I handled.
Whiffing the baby
smeared with my smell,
she won't take back my child.

Margaret Hasse

Years ago, in the 1970s, I was featured with four other Twin Cities women poets in a magazine article. The cover photograph showed a woman, her face in shadows, in a garret-like space, writing in a notebook. Some poets I knew railed against this media image of the pristine poetess, sequestered away from the world, in her privacy, disengaged. People took umbrage because the picture seemed so ethereal, the poet so separate from audience, politics and the world.

While I understood this point of view, I was and remain attached to the picture of the woman in the attic. For all my grown-up life—and even when I was an adolescent with an avid taste for Dickinson and James Dickey—I've tried to maintain my own garret for poetry.

I write because I need to. Poetry is the most generous source of profound spiritual experience I know. It's also an act in which I take great pleasure. Sometimes, however, I've struggled with my own allotment of talent, disparaging it, wishing it were more. Terrible dust covered my desk during several periods in my life. Yet I've always returned, needing to be a member of poetry's tribe, needing to know I was developing what I had in me.

I live my life in a small hubbub of physical and social energy—volunteering at school, holding jobs, staying involved with family and friends. A physical room stands in for, reflects and protects my commitment to disciplined and usually solitary meditation on life, experience and words. It's where I read, write, make associations between my life and imagination and the world of concrete images and of rhythm and sound. It's where I am most in touch with my forebears—actual ancestors and literary ones.

Poetry writing always requires a sheaf of poems, a stack of books written by others. To be genuinely engaged in poetry means not only attending to one's own inner life. It also means taking on what others have done, learning from other poems and poets, and making many poems that suggest and imitate and relate to those on whose shoulders we stand.

(Photo by Lonnie Knutson)

Anthony Swann has been writing poetry since childhood. His work has appeared in many small publications and newspapers, and he has read at coffeehouses located in places as diverse as Bemidji, the Twin Cities, and Las Vegas. "The first poetry readings I attended in the 60's," he says, "were held in the Extempore coffeehouse at its original location at Cedar/Riverside in Minneapolis, which had originally been a jazz coffeehouse which a black artist friend and I founded called 'The Broken Drum.' The Extempore kept music as its focus. I heard poets like Franklin Brainerd and Michael Kincaid there, and the readings were hosted by James Naiden, editor of the *North Stone Review*. The poets could improvise like the musicians with a freedom of expression. I was also a member of the Lake Street Writers Group, which I remember fondly."

A jazz afficionado and student of Latin American culture and music, Swann is currently working on a novel about jazz people and artists. He lives in Bemidji, Minnesota.

These Are My People

These are my people
the jazz babies
the hangers on
second liners
the thrill kids
on or off the sauce
who hang around the funk-pit clubs at night,
saxophones soaring like hawks
a slo-gin slow blues pouring out the door
into nights of carnal *film-noire* pleasure
and backed-up cold turkey pain,
on their runs or comin' off
moving like animated panthers,
loose-jointed Mick Jaggers,
Symphony Sids on the prowl,
looking for kicks
but mostly the good deep pleasure
in The Sound, The Holy Sound, man,
that came outa the Big Easy, Chi-town, St. Louis, Memphis,
52nd St., and K.C., man, and moved into the
heart of a country too white and full of hate
to see a good thing on bargain basement vinyl
and Duke Ellington went unrecognized until
his sophistication just overcame it all,
and The Count came over the radio
and later Miles and Mingus prowled stages like shamans
all focused on The Sound, The Holy Sound.

These are my people
comin' in to hear the music and have a beer
to cram loins in lusty dance
or just relax, rap, share and signify.
Yes, these are my people
and the blues in the night,
a long lost train thru America that's comin' home,
that's my music.

Anthony Swann

The Outpost

Fame or money
aren't on the outpost
where empty winds howl loudly
over open snow-swept spaces
where desolation
sets in good
and solitude is your only recognition.
If you come here for adventure
you will find other things first
and like the empty coffee cans
in the trappers' cabins
you will be useless for a time . . .

The outpost
is known only to the wolves
who howl in the bitter depths of frozen winter nights,
to the bush-batty, stir-crazy trappers and loners.
There is nothing but the empty howl of the wind,
and long hard cold.

You have to have gone over these life and death distances,
traversed the space
to feel the extraordinary harmony
of the outpost,
the silence . . .
and no tracks in the snow.

Anthony Swann

Beethoven Mad in the Streets

Beethoven mad in the streets
cursing mumbling to himself like Steppenwolf
hung over and freshly drunk on wine
stumbling on litter
food particles on his expensive but smelly
week-old clothes
hair unkept

people stare at Beethoven
peg him an alcoholic stumble bum
he shouts at them or ignores them
walks on aimlessly
his hoary head buzzin' full of melodies immortal
ideas he turns into masterpieces
later falling womanless into an unkept bed,
angels watching over him as he snores.

Wild Rice, Wild Roses

Oh soul
you will never see
all the acres of earth,
never the quaint patterns of life
peculiar to certain treks of land,
never all the hidden stages of earth,
their unknown productions,
nor mark what breathes or worships the sun
in those foreign places.

Yes, you have your own altar,
that it be hallowed the greatest,
and I ask what right you have
to think your corner more holy,
being only a grain of the earth,
when everywhere, every place, is an altar.
Those pasture grasses that lie inviting in the heat of noon,
those Aztec reaches of jungle heights,
and all the forbidden valleys you'll never see,
nor suddenly come out upon some field in spring
and hear the life there sing,
budding, blooming, exalting life you'll never see.

Anthony Swann

A Homeless Person Arranges His Belongings

At a bus stop a homeless person arranges his belongings
accommodating a new winter hat and scarf
the mission gave out after the Thanksgiving feast
televised LIVE,
a camera scanning them all
focusing an invading eye on the more picturesque
like old black men with white beards
and the Mayor with the homeless on his one side
and mission big shots who have dressed up on his other side.
Eating in silence our homeless person watched
some of the homeless duck the camera or leave early,
embarrassed that relatives in real homes might be watching.
One said, "If I want my dad to see me I'll send him a picture!"
      "What would you like to drink?" asks a neat,
        charming lady server, "coffee, juice or milk?"
      "MILK!" shouts one fellow, "It's good for a body,
        that an' Wonder Bread!"

Sun pours in on the bus stop.
The near zero chill of air has gone
and the homeless person takes off a layer of his shirts,
his bones now warm.
He has achieved a moment of complete unselfconsciousness
and without a trace of anger for the stares
of people wanting a bus but refusing to sit by him
he folds his blanket smaller, stuffing it into his pack
beside
        a second pair of jeans
        a second shirt
        dirty socks
        some bread, a spoon, pocketknife
        plastic plate and cup,
        small jar of instant coffee
        and two photos in a small worn fold-up frame,
        one of a relative long dead,
        another of a woman still alive but 2000 miles away.

Anthony Swann

He moves his pack out into the sunlight
to join The Sacred Army of the Homeless
in the next soup line,
soup and starch, always lots of starch . . .
His hair is white, his body light,
his mind light too, like a child's mind
still easily amused by the pigeons scurrying for the bread in the
    mission yard,
the same pigeons the crazies chase and curse
remind him of the Wright brothers testing the air at Kittyhawk
and the Vietnam and Desert Storm boys
remind him of poppies in Flander's Field.

At night before sleep blesses him, or at dawn when it leaves,
amid the snores, farts and groans from bunk beds
or a blanket-width above cold hard rocky ground
he has had visions which sometimes come to pass.
"The good one," he says. "I might tell ya,
the bad ones I keep to myself."

I chose to leave college after my junior year feeling *I could learn more about writing in the work-a-day world than on campus. This decision was valid then, but now I envy the knowledge and articulateness of English teachers. I have supported myself as a cook and at other menial jobs. However, I once taught English in Brazil in a second language school and to private students during an extended stay there.*

Afro-American and Latin music has influenced my writing and kept me emotionally alive during the 50's, which I felt were an extremely sterile time for a creative person to survive. The poetry which excites me the most is from spiritual texts, especially Bengali songs and Hindu texts, because of the powerful truths therein and the beauty of their inspired expression.

As a boy I likened the poetic impulse to a heron by the river and I made pilgrimages to the heron's secret spot. To observe it I had to execute formidable stealth. The heron had a magical awareness attuned to the natural world like a sentinel of perception standing in the river of the flux of time. I thrilled when I read the passages in James Joyce's Portrait of the Artist as a Young Man *where Stephen Daedalus realizes an identification with his self-generated image of "the hawklike man whose name he bore soaring out of his captivity on osierwoven wings." Joyce's symbol of the man-bird was culled from his inner life and a need for a symbol to represent a calling of its own beyond the mundane world of human society, its commercial concerns and organized religions. I realized that the heron was my personal symbol for this same calling. I would have Picasso paint the heron with an oversized eye as a symbol of perception. The heron's flight on its huge wings is totally majestic.*

Anthony Swann

Gary Holthaus credits his father for planting the poetic seed. "I have loved reading poems since I was a child," he recalls. "Pop read to my brother and me, each of us seated on the living room couch on either side of him. Pop read everything from Wordsworth to the Hoosier poet, Shakespeare, Whittier and Frost." Holthaus has authored several collections including *Unexpected Manna* (Copper Canyon Press, 1978) and *Circling Back* (Gibbs Smith, 1984). He also has a collection of essays, *Wide Skies: Finding a Home in the West* (University of Arizona Press, 1997).

Currently Holthaus is the principal of *words into focus*, a consulting firm that works with non-profits. He lives in Red Wing, Minnesota.

Brother

(For Jack)

What I remember
is sleeping
both in the same room
sometimes in the same bed.

And what I remember
sleeping
is sleeping with my arm
around you, holding
the small years close.

Of waking I remember:

Standing in the kitchen doorway
when they brought you home;
Mother on a gurney,
me in corduroy knickers
and high-top boots
with a knife on the side.

The time I took you to the basement,
my chore to take the clinkers out,
and you saw the furnace tongs
glowing red hot and beautiful
as some inverted tulip
you reached to pluck . . .

Later, you decided
to go on your own, plunging
down the cement steps to the cellar,
your walker ricocheting off the wall,
through the glass door at the bottom.

Eyes wide with shattering
we ran to find you
calm and silent, without a cut.

Gary Holthaus

The summer
(were you only 14?)
you nearly lost a finger
to a buzz saw in Colorado
working for Rileys
and I smashed mine,
same finger on the same hand,
between two I-beams at Iowa Steel.
When you left the bus that fall
neither of us could shake hands
and we laughed and laughed . . .

But the everyday dilemmas:
marriages, divorce, children growing—
how you fared then
and in the work you've had,
and what made you what you are
I'll never know;
the working years have kept us far
from knowing well the ways we've gone.

So now,
when we're together, I watch
and try to backtrack where you've been
and how you got to where you are
and look to find myself as well,

And wonder if, beyond the hurts
we all are heir to
the years between us ever will grow
small and close
before we sleep again.

Gary Holthaus

Blouse

I wanted to tell you
earlier, this afternoon,
but didn't know how, quite,
and there wasn't time
at the time . . .

So I'll tell you now
what I thought then:

That's a beautiful blouse
you have on, pink as the pink
on the inside of your lips,
and never more beautiful than now:

You pulling it over your head
with all four of our hands,
letting it fall to the floor
in the hall.

Gary Holthaus

What It Comes Down To

If I could
anchor myself
here
and go down
deeper and deeper
in this one
place

a time would
come, perhaps
when I could
penetrate
even this unyielding
indifferent earth,
find here
what remains
unknown:

a name
for that nameless
absence
we seek to fill

an end
or point
to our own long
absence
from home.

Gary Holthaus

An Archaeology of History

My history is my identity.
—Ossie Davis

Knowing what we know,
knowing what we do for ourselves
will disappear,
knowing only what we do in love
will last
we watch our loved ones walk away
into stories, into shadows
so deep
we cannot see or follow.

    And the rest—
that unknown woman passing on the street
who appears to be so nice
we want to say, "Wait . . .!"
even in this city of alien speech . . .

And you, to whom I have nothing
to give, no easier way; or this stranger
with inquiring eye, these old men
with no place to go—

Czeslaw, you are right:
the passionless cannot change history.
But neither can the passionate
alter that ultimate midden heaped
at the edge of our city
pressing against the walls.

We sift through it seeking to create
the artifacts we had hoped to find,
knowing it will take our life
to shape the find we desire.

See
even the old men with no place to go
are hurrying toward it.

Gary Holthaus

The Barn

In this dream the barn
settles into its own crumbling,
returning to earth where
Blackhawk once led his band
down the river to fish or war.

Inside, sunlight falls
through the broken-shingled roof,
rides the backs of Belgians, both
standing hipshot in their stalls.
Shadows under their necks
stretch across the manger.

One flicks at a fly.

One swings his heavy head back
to nip at his own withers. Oats
dribble to the floor.

The first fear I remember—
Was I only two and unsure of foot?—
The only percheron on the place came
dancing roof high around the corner
just as I, like an old man
stepping
over a low retaining wall,
tottered over the oak threshhold
into the bright uncertain world
directly into his flowing path,
looking for Grandpa.

Gary Holthaus

When I first drove into Red Wing a few years back, I thought, "I know this country..." Everything from my childhood is here: the oaks and maples, their latent flare of color in the coming fall; the high limestone bluffs brooding above the Mississippi; the Mississippi itself, the sloughs and backwaters that are part of its spreading across the broad valley and help give that river such a sense of flowing presence and brooding power; cottontails and rattlesnakes and cardinals and bluejays. Pheasants in the cornfields and barpits. The long rows of corn that would surely be knee-high by the Fourth, the clean rows of beans. Watercress, milkweed, sumac. The names of things were all around me like poems. I grew up in Iowa, but had not lived in a Midwest landscape for years. Yet it came back in a flood of memory. It wasn't like coming home, but a return to the familiar. I could learn it again, the connection to it was instant.

Poems began to come again too. The images of the surrounding landscape began to insert themselves—barns, sloughs, draft horses, red oaks—the more subtle to come later.

I try to write my own poems because I enjoy, —no, because I love—the process. I share some with friends, and sometimes one gets published. But that is not the point. The point is to write them, and to be caught up again in that rush and excitement when a phrase or line strikes the mind with a cadence that cannot be ignored.

For me, the form of a poem is always negotiable. There is a difference between starting with a form and pouring a poem into it, and starting with a line that wants to become a poem and letting it grow into its own form. If one is committed to form, then the search begins for an appropriate form, perhaps one that immediately matches the meter of the line. If one is committed instead to the words or the idea or the cadence, one may put them down, let them steep, find a form or devise a form as the lines grow.

The former is the method, not to be spurned, of the person who builds the foundation of our house; the latter is that of a sculptor before a block of marble. Both let something be realized. One pours (at worst, forces) the creation into a foreign vessel; the latter sets his creation free. Both are makers.

CarolAnn Marie Russell grew up in Bozeman, Montana, and Detroit Lakes, Minnesota. Her studies of poetry at the University of Montana and University of Nebraska, which allowed her to work with writers such as Richard Hugo, Tess Gallagher, and Greg Kuzma, grounded her in a writing life that includes teaching at the State University of Minnesota at Bemidji. Since 1985 she has published three full-length collections—*The Red Envelope* (University Presses of Florida), *Feast* (Loonfeather Press) and *Silver Dollar* (West End Press)—and has distinguished herself by winning several awards. In 1997 and 2000 she spent time as a Visiting Artist at the American Academy in Rome, Italy. A bi-lingual collection of new poems, *Italia,* was presented in Cagliari, Verona, Rome and Florence.

Poets of the *Cimitero Acattolico*

I take the number thirteen bus
To the end of the line
To find you. A pyramid
Burns white in December sun,
Opening the inner door
To all who follow. Your
Guardians are the cats of Rome.
Free as your soul and fed
Without obligation or regret,
They pad outside the Aurelian Wall
Washing their feet
In leftover rain. A black one,
His tail dipped white
I call "Resurrection" and follow
To the gate where, taking a deep breath
I pull the iron bell.
Three times I ring
Before someone comes.
Three times I have nearly died,
My heart on the ground
And three times
Brought back to the knife edge.
In this, the miniature city of the dead,
Beauty wears a strange face,
Frozen, a stone angel
Among earth's rich green.
A tiger cat is waiting
Where I sit near Shelley's tomb,
Rubbing his whiskered face
Against my thigh, pawing
My leather jacket. He stands
Motionless in salute, his nose
Pointing toward the open door
Of the tower. I follow his gaze
To the other side where a young tree grows.
Now your benedictions
Are Italian, freely given
By those who come

CarolAnn Russell

To remember what song is,
How it bursts the gates of anger or joy,
Flaming heart
At the heart of things
That keeps us human
And in love. What we give
Abundantly death cannot
Barter nor gain—
Our mortal celebration
Like sunlit rain through cloud,
A cellular flowing from,
A river to the sea-change
Without need for a single coin
To bring us home. Come,
Blow a kiss with me
To the ashes
The beautiful bodies
Death has dazzled into sleep
And dance upon the leaden shield.

Hotel Excelsior

Campania, con panna e compagnia

I fall into my own heart
In love with *Tasso* and *San Francesco*,
Siren in gold and silver
Sandals walking the streets,
Touching *orchideas*
As boys throw firecrackers
Off the cliff
Into turquoise
Jewels of *Amalfi*
Set in platinum dusk.
Across the Tyhrennian Sea
The breast of Vesuvius
Floats danger like cream.
I open Italian doors
And run the bath hot
Slipping naked
Beneath the foam.
Blushing at the waiter,
Barely twenty, who brings me
Two glasses slipped between his fingers
And a bottle of chilled *chianti*.
The sea sings a deep song.

CarolAnn Russell

Last Judgment at Orvieto

On a slow train from Rome I fall in love
The way Italians do
When money's tight and fountains
Fail to run. The streets can stink
For all I care: the war my father fought
Is over. I am humming
Elvis Presley—"Love Me Tender"
To a man across the aisle.
We are both on leave from the past,
No longer foreign to *fortuna*,
Speaking Spanish
To confound the Fates.

The "O" on his belt-buckle
Gleams silver, Argentine
For Orvieto. I twist
The diamond deeper into flesh.
No reason except a woman
And a man. Tonight
We'll climb medieval streets
Cobbled by pain
To where sun fires tufa stone
And bells rock against the towers
To say we are alive

Enough to suffer dawn
And walls collapsed
Around our hearts.
Not just sex as puritans think
But loveliness,
The beauty of somebody's
Absolute imperfection
Held the moment
All is shaken
When the light we are
Begs to shine.

Scala Del Bovolo

Islands in a bruised lagoon
Sink into ooze, an inch each year
You're lonely.
Bound by vows to water
You are twice his age—it doesn't matter.
Trust gravity will hold you
When you fall. Whirl

A silken cape about your shoulders,
And thumb your nose at plagues—
Blood-kiss behind a fan.
Each pink *palazzo* is a wedding cake
For poets, mirrored upside down
In gorgeous sludge. Wrap your persona
In leopard skin and lace
So she can flirt, unmask herself
On the *vaporetto* with a handsome man
Who restores paintings.
Birds lift off and sail
Clear to *Murano* and die
Luminous in glass.

Repeat after me, "not guilty"
And cross the Bridge of Sighs.
Piombi or *Ca-Dario*, you know better
Than tell a lie in Harry's Bar
So far from home. All is booty
For the hungry soul. Drink
To stone lions who guard virginity
Of whores. Leave lost wars
And accusations in their mouths
And sing yourself an aria
Before you climb
The ancient spiral into air.

CarolAnn Russell

Incarnation

No passive virgin this woman
Whose countenance graced banners—
Moslem and Christian—crusading
Both sides of sin. Her genius
Like that of Janus, two-faced
Imperfectly divined: the amniotic sea
And devil's gateway, deserter
Of the tree and water.
Tertullian craftsmen covered her hands
To hide the dirt beneath
Her nails,
And pearly semen on her legs.
No celibate queen
But *primadonna* for a jealous God
She's since walked out on.
I imagine her on a *moto*
Cruising the cosmos
In search of a lover
Who likes to dance,
Teaching love: what is,
Is heaven enough.

CarolAnn Russell

I remember distinctly the first few times *I realized poetry as a power in my life, a dynamic source. Once, in 1963 when an English teacher, Mrs. Dolphay, spontaneously recited, with unrestrained drama "Gunga Din" for the seventh grade class; then, 1968 in Australia, when Mr. McGregor, the English Master in Literature, recited long sections from* King Lear *under magnolia trees on the green; and again in 1975 when Richard Hugo recited "The Lady in Kicking Horse Reservoir" after telling us how he wrote the poem in a fit of jealousy, realizing it would be better to "kill" the faithless female in a really good poem rather than hunting her down with a revolver.*

Each of these memories resides somewhere in my body, an intricate pattern of sound become feeling become thought which continues to refine who I am becoming. More than anything, poetry is for me an acculturating force, psychic and generative, which fills me like a reservoir and from which I continually draw in living and in making art. Certain poems wait for me like beautiful rooms or mysterious persons, with absolute faith that eventually I will come to know them. Others emerge volcanically, on the edge of passion or terror, from deep chasms. Conscious or unconscious, the poem teaches more intensely than any form I know the art of returning to the source of raw feeling to reclaim awareness and respect for the lived, individual life. Complexity, intensity, paradox, harmony and what Yeats called "terrible beauty" are all the fruits of poetry.

For me, poetry is not a product of imagination but a generative language, thought married to feeling. Poetry is the music of being fully present in one's life, friend and family and lover of the world. Writing and reading poetry have given me a way to love the world, deeply and unafraid. Every poem I write is a love poem, connected to a real passion for some person or place, a moment of recognition which leads me away from and back to my true and perfectly impure life.

The poets I know and love are all passionate to live (and write) the ever present now, where craziness and failure can be mourned without judgment, then forgiven and redeemed. Yes, poetry has saved my life; the paradox is that at the same time poetry has eaten my life. It's a mortal love, this one, dangerous and real.

(Photo by Michael Hardwick)

As a graduate student in environmental engineering, **Scott King** has had the opportunity to study the land and numerous lakes in northeastern Minnesota. By seeking to "tie the natural world to the inner world, religion to politics, or even economics to autumn," his life and poetry converge.

Born in Bemidji, he grew up in Pelican Rapids near the shores of Lake Lida and went to college in Duluth and Minneapolis. He has worked in Cass Lake and in several suburbs, and now resides in Northfield where he works as a printer and editor for Red Dragonfly Press. His poetry has appeared in several small literary journals.

"My metaphors," he says, "are Minnesotan."

At the Shore of Snowbank Lake

"Search in your heart
for the sun that has left."
—**Yannis Ritsos**

This would be a good place to look for the bones of poets,
the ones who had no paper, who knew what it was like
to speak through holes in the wind,
a good place to listen to the wind filling up the silence,
clamoring over the deadfalls of a brutal century.
I stand here and only watch as seagulls
gather up remnants of shattered light off the waves,
watch the sun crumbling at the horizon, knowing soon
the moon will come and place its hands in this lake
in order to rinse the blood from its bandages.
I was born with a war in my eyes, so it is easy
to imagine ashes dissolved in this lake's clear water
like sugar or the taste of glaciers, easy to imagine
the long sound of rocks being ground to sand.
This is a strange place, however peaceful, however isolate,
where trees freeze upright in winter unable to bend
to the sun, a strange place where the stars have labored
thousands of years to wear these grooves in the rock, here,
where the one road ends in water.
I look at all the yellowed leaves steeping in puddles.
I watch the pale eyelids of the dozing lichen,
I notice the spider webs that buttress the ruins of autumn,
the strewn desolation of the forest's floor.
I study the bleached and rusting claws of crayfish.
I catch myself living in the moment's decay.
Now five or six snowflakes come down from the clear sky
and I realize I have no gods to invoke, nothing but
this solitude, a single loon calling
somewhere between the sun and a tiny minnow of moon,
somewhere between all the stars and drowning,
as though it had carved a whistle out of my bones.

Scott King

What It's Like

It's early spring. A young boy sits in the ditch by a gravel road watching
    water spill from the mouth of a metal culvert.
He waits for something to float out of that dark tunnel.
A tiny fragment of a cattail blade goes by submerged in the tea-stained
    water, spinning and tumbling in the current.
Then a pencil drifts out like a splinter off the original cross.
Then, a styrofoam cup with a piece bitten from its rim.
Strange, he thinks to himself, but wonderful as well.
And just before he leaves, a fresh-cut daffodil emerges—
surely this is the flag of some far-off and future country. Later,
after the sun has set and the boy has closed his eyes in sleep, the stars
    will swim there, in the pool beneath the culvert, like newly-hatched
    minnows.

The Hill

Often he returns to the hill that houses his mother's ashes.
He stands there, empty as a hand. He tries to understand
    the blades of grass sawing at his knees,
tries to understand the smell of distant hay and lake water.
He is conscious of his hair above the land like leaves
    sprung from the tortured oak.
The moment always contains both day and night.
With his tongue, he is trying to feel the inside of his skull.
He knows that this tangle of stars is somehow in his head
and that any meaning is really quite simple, like the moment's
unexplained sumac trees and maples or the mysterious cattail
to which a red-winged blackbird keeps returning and returning.
A land of humid shadows and greenish winds in summer,
a hill of frigid noise and star-lit bones in winter, he stands
    there,
one foot in spring the other in autumn, trying to understand.

Todos Santos

November 1, 1998

1

Early morning. I stand outside in the frost,
in front of a small apartment, calling
for my vagrant cat. A chickadee hops up
empty branches in the nearby crabapple tree
hoping for food at my empty hands. Though poor
I'm no Saint Francis, the chickadee flies away
and I can only hope the cat comes back.
I stand exhaling fleeting clouds of breath,
remembering my mother and how she woke
one morning just long enough to say goodbye.

2

Late afternoon. The sun at the horizon,
its last rays lighting the leaves like candles,
leading me farther away from my home.
Late dragonflies hustle to mate, cellophane wings
flashing over ragged, wind-blown weeds.
A belief of some kind, something wind won't wear down,
finds me at the cemetery's edge holding an empty milkweed pod.
I sit down, place my bare hands upon the dead ground,
and watch a distant oak fill with crows. The sun's final glimpse
of this world turning the tree's few leaves as dark and bright
as I might hold the word "love" upon my tongue.

The Dark after Autumn

(For Evan Robert Walker)

September reaped the sunshine of fiery August
And October came down in a flood of Leaves.
Now it's November and it rains and rains.
    We have given you our Light.

Our years are propped against the Millennium,
And wars go on, economies falter like old hearts,
But you are safe, born into this circle, this plenum of Friends.
    We have given you our Lives.

All night the rain fell in puddles. This morning
We kneel and trace the cross in our cold reflections.
At church it rains again, dripping from God's fingertips.
    We have given you our Beliefs.

When winter comes and stares hard at our windows
Like a page out of the Bible, when Leaves grow dark
Beneath the snow, and the black covers keep you warm,
Open your eyes onto our Season, bless our leaning faces,
    And give us your Light.

An Old Language

    This morning, the wind and a bent weed
    working together . . .

    drawing the shape of last night's moon
    in the snow.

Metaphor provides complication, demands an intimacy *with the world, and, like a disturbance on the surface of quiet water, catches our eyes. Some poems are fused from so many metaphors that they come before our eyes as intricate and patterned as Damascus steel. Others hold up to the reader a single, perfect metaphor, the poet as proud as a child who has caught a snowflake on the tip of one finger.*

There seem to be enough species for an army of botanists with pins and collection bottles, enough to launch a new branch of the sciences, identifying and studying the life and habitat of metaphor. In the absence of a systematic approach, we are left mainly with superstitions, trial and error. Even so, we are not without hope, for there are many poets (and novelists) who have mastered the craft of metaphor, and we can learn from them as we attempt to salvage and unearth from our own lives metaphor, and reinvent and fashion from the unlikeliness of this world and our living, poems.

Acknowledgments

Richards, Melanie: "Maps of the Lost Kingdom," and "Nerval's Raven," in *Minnesota Monthly*, February, 1995. "Solace of an Evening Lit by Streetlights," in *Minnesota Monthly*, September, 1994. "Dream of the Salamander," in *Mythos Journal*, Fall, 1992. "White Tigers," in *Kalliope*, Vol. XVII, #2, 1995.

Hardy, Rob: "River Bend," in *Cannon River Watershed Watcher*, November, 1997. "Morning," in *Black Bear Review*, Spring, 2000. "Instructions for Silent Prayer," in *The Comstock Review*, Vol. 13, #2, 1999.

McCarthy, Eugene: "The Public Man," "Three Bad Signs," "Kilroy," "Vietnam Message," "Quiet Waters," "Place of Promise," and "Grant Park, Chicago," in *Selected Poems*, Lone Oak Press, 1997. Statement excerpts from *The Year of the People*, Doubleday, 1969.

Prefontaine, Joan Wolf: "Earth Tones," in *Minnesota Poetry Calendar*, Black Hat Press, 1998. "Raspberries," and "Tornado Salad," in *Loonfeather*, Fall/Winter, 1991. "Choreography," in *Loonfeather*, Vol. 17, #1, 1996. "Early Planting," in *Poem*, 1981.

Togeas, James: "September Fog," in *Sundog*, 1991. "Comet," in *The Hale Bopp Poetry Collection*, 1997. "Angel of Belief," in *Sundog*, 1986.

McKay, Linda Back: "Night Measures," in *Loonfeather*, Vol. 17, #1, 1996. "Indian Cemetery," in *North Coast Review*, #3, 1993. "Dislocated Worker Project," in *California Quarterly*, 1998. "Responsibility," in *Loonfeather*, Summer, 1998.

Richard Broderick: "Equinox," in *The Lucid Stone*, 1991. "The Mountains of Florida," in *Smartish Pace*, 2000. "Moonrise over Lake Michigan," in *Talking River Review*, 1996. "Sundays Spent Working at Home," in *Troubador*, 1998. "Swimming Laps," in *The Atlantic Review*, 2000.

Barnes, Debra: "Out of Time," in *ArtWord Quarterly*, Fall, 1999. "Marriage at 42 Below," in *The Formalist*, Vol. 10, #2. "The Transcendence of Poetry," in *ArtWord Quarterly*, Spring, 1998.

Kincaid, Michael: "Northern Solstice," in *Voices*, b. ginaviv press, 1993. "Lunar Function," in *Cave Light*, Midcontinent Press, 1985. "Hymn to Otherness," in *Vagrant Deity*, Salvage Press, 1999. "Good Manners," in *Mythos Journal*, Winter, 1995.

Dittberner-Jax, Norita: "Sauerkraut Supper," in *Hurricane Alice*, 1994. "Senior English," in *Minnesota Monthly*, May, 1998. "West Seventh Street," in *Border Crossings*, New Rivers Press, 1984.

Whitledge, Jane: "The Doll's Head," in *Plains Poetry Journal,* April, 1986. "Morel Mushrooms," in *Wilderness,* Spring, 1993.

Schild, Steven: "Beatitude: Cycle of Water," in *ArtWord Quarterly,* Summer, 1997. "Sandwiches After the Service," in *Whiskey Island Magazine,* Fall, 1994. "The Bride," in *Wolf Head Quarterly,* Autumn, 1996. "Heirlooms," in *Minnesota Poetry Calendar,* Black Hat Press, 1998.

Heideman, Kathleen: "Lost Gospel of Infancy," publication pending in *Yefief.* "Villanelle for a Negaunee Oracle," in *Explorations,* 1998. "Signs and Signifiers," in *Minnesota Poetry Calendar,* Black Hat Press, 2000.

Browne, Michael Dennis: "Evensong," in *Tri-Quarterly,* 1989. "The Now, The Long Ago," in *Selected Poems,* 1996. "Mengele," in *The Iowa Review,* 1986. "Hide and Seek," in *Aspen Anthology,* 1980.

Lund, Orval: "Plowing," "For John Who Did Not Choose Baseball," "Take Paradise," and "Men in Winter," in *Casting Lines,* New Rivers Press, 1999.

Meissner, Bill: "Secrets of America," in *Sleepwalker's Son,* Ohio University Press, 1987.

McKiernan, Ethna: "Homage to the Common," in *Sidewalks.* "The Other Woman," in *Caravan,* 1989. "Those We Carry With Us," in *Minnesota Monthly.* "At This Moment," in *Minnesota Poetry Calendar,* Black Hat Press, 2001.

Hedin, Robert: "The Snow Country," "Waiting for Trains at Col D'Aubisque," "Bells," "Goddard Hot Springs," and "The Old Liberators," in *The Old Liberators,* Holy Cow! Press, 1998.

Broderson, Lucille: "White Milk at Daybreak," in *Tri-Quarterly.* "Harvested Field," in *Agassiz Review,* Vol 2, #1, Spring, 1991. "This is Your Old Age, Lucy," in *Poetry.*

Youngblom, Tracy: "Joseph" in *Kansas Quarterly,* Vol. 26, #1-4, 1994. "O Earthly Zion," in *Shenandoah,* Vol. 42, #4, Winter, 1992.

McCullough, Ken: "Instructions (for Shivani Arjuna)," and "Visitation," in *Travelling Light,* Thunder's Mouth Press, 1987. "Finishing Merrill Gilfillan . . .," in *Minnesota Poetry Calendar,* Black Hat Press, 2001. "The Red and Black," in *The Iowa Source.* "Run, Late November," in *Nimrod.* "Instructions (for Galway McCullough)," in *Sycamore,* Oriole, 1991.

Sutphen, Joyce: "Crossroads," "From Out the Cave," and "My Father Comes to the City," in *Straight Out of View,* Beacon Press, 1995. "Launching into Space," and "Comforts of the Sun," in *Coming Back to the Body,* Holy Cow! Press, 2000. "Casino," in *Atlanta Review,* Fall/Winter, 1998.

Dacey, Philip: "She Writes Offering to Buy for Her Son . . .," "Walt Whitman's Answering Service," and "Nomen, Numen," all reprinted with permission of the author.

Rummel, Mary Kay: "Sonata," in *Northeast,* Juniper Press, 2000. "Medieval Herbal," in *Water-Stone,* Fall, 2000. "In the Night Kitchen," in *The Long Journey Into North,* Juniper Press, 1998.

Hewett, Greg: "The Distance to Birth," in *The American Literary Review*.

Downes, Claire van Breemen: "Mulberry Creek," in *Lake Street Review,* Winter, 1985-86. "A Double Sonnet . . .," in *NFSPS Prize Poems,* 1996.

Hasse, Margaret: "Grave," in *Midwest Quarterly,* 1999. "Bean Fields," in *The Talking of Hands,* New Rivers Press, 1998. "A Favorite Dessert, Lips," in *Stars Above, Stars Below,* New Rivers Press, 1984. "Marking Him," in *Touched by Adoption,* Green River Press, 1999.

Swann, Anthony: "These are My People," in *North Coast Review,* Summer, 1998.

Holthaus, Gary: "Brother," "What It Comes Down To," and "An Archaeology of History," in *An Archaeology of Home,* Limberlost Press, 1998. "Blouse," in *If You Were Here I Would Have Hands,* Brooding Heron Press, 1999.

Russell, CarolAnn Marie: "Poets of the *Cimitero Acattolico,*" in *Notre Dame Review,* Winter, 2000.

King, Scott: "At the Shore of Snowbank Lake," in *Pemmican,* 1996. "The Hill," in *Lake Region Review,* 1998.